Elevate
FATHERHOOD
Measuring What Matters Most

Marland May MS

Inks and Bindings
888-290-5218
www.inksandbindings.com
orders@inksandbindings.com

Join the Elevate Fatherhood community for exclusive content, discussions, and support.

Get fatherhood gear that represents your commitment to being the best dad you can be.

Access resources designed to help you grow, lead, and leave a lasting legacy.

Visit ElevateFatherhood.com to join the community and gear up today!

Table of Contents

Part 3

Mastering Emotional Intelligence
Navigating Emotions with Kids
Modeling Emotional Teaching
The Power of Play

Part 4

Fostering Lifelong Learning
The Art of Attachment styles
Foundations of Trust and Connection
Establish a Legendary Legacy

Forward

Every year around Father's Day, I feel uneasy, especially when I see T-shirts in stores exaggerating claims about
being the "greatest dad in the world." To earn the title of
the greatest of all time (GOAT), there must be a measure-
ment scale and, perhaps even more critically, a competition
where one can truly stand out.

Fatherhood is more than just a role; it is a calling. It's
an unspoken commitment to be present for your children,
nurturing, guiding, and preparing them for the world's beauty and challenges. Yet, the journey of fatherhood is rarely
straightforward. Although no two paths are alike, one truth
unites us all: fatherhood is transformative.

When I became a father to triplets, my life took an
unexpected and exhilarating turn. I found myself standing

at the crossroads of chaos and joy, wrestling with questions I didn't yet have answers to. How do I nurture three unique individuals while also maintaining my own identity? How do I balance the demands of work, relationships, and parenthood? How do I raise kind, confident, and resilient children? These questions, along with my background in counseling, education, and personal development, inspired me to create a framework that lies at the heart of this book. This framework revolves around four key pillars of fatherhood:

1. **Play** – Building bonds through joy and imagination.
2. **Emotional Intelligence** – Modeling empathy, emotional regulation, and connection.
3. **Attachment Style**– Creating trust and stability in your child's world.
4. **Lifelong Learning** – Cultivating curiosity and growth for yourself and your children.

When I became a father to triplets, my life took an unexpected and exhilarating turn. Overnight, I transitioned from dreaming about fatherhood to navigating its realities at triple speed. Questions swirled in my mind like a tornado cutting across the Midwest plains: How do I nurture three unique individuals while maintaining my own identity? How do I balance work, relationships, and parenting? Am I doing a good job—or could I do better?

The stakes became painfully honest when, just months after coming home from the NICU, two of my daughters were hospitalized with RSV. Their tiny bodies fought valiantly, but the experience left me questioning every decision I'd made. It was the holidays, and more family members wanted to see the kids. We were strict about hygiene and health, even before COVID. Yet they still became dreadfully sick. Was I already falling short as a father?

As these questions troubled me, I realized I couldn't afford to wait ten years to find out if I was on the right path. I needed to know now if I was doing enough and if I was growing in the ways my children needed. That led me to something I have always trusted: metrics.

I have always been comfortable with metrics and statistics—precise, measurable tools that provide a roadmap and hold me accountable. Whether tracking progress at work or pursuing personal goals, numbers have offered me a way to assess, adjust, and grow. It seemed only natural to seek a similar system to guide me in my journey as a father.

Thus, the concept of Key Performance Indicators (KPIs) for fathers was born. This approach allows me to measure not only where I currently stand but also where I need to go, helping me navigate the twists and turns of parenting with clarity and purpose.

In business, Key Performance Indicators (KPIs) are measurable values used to assess progress toward goals. They foster clarity and accountability in environments that demand consistent growth and adaptability.Fatherhood isn't different. KPIs for fathers aren't metrics meant to judge;

they're principles to help you reflect on your progress, identify areas for growth, and celebrate where you're succeeding. This book will introduce you to the four key pillars of fatherhood, offering practical tools, real-life stories, and actionable strategies to help you elevate your journey.

Every father starts at a different place on this path. Some of us are naturally nurturing, while others are still learning how to express love or set boundaries. This book isn't about creating a "perfect father"—that doesn't exist. It's about helping you become the best father you can be, given your unique circumstances and strengths.

Legendary fathers are not born; they're made. Any father can reach this level of connection and impact through reflection, intentionality, and a willingness to learn. Whether you're changing your first diaper, coaching your child through life's challenges, or watching them graduate into adulthood, the principles in this book will serve as your compass. They'll help you navigate the highs and lows of fatherhood with clarity, confidence, and connection.

My goal is to revolutionize how Father's Day is celebrated in the decades to come. I want to honor those who are on the journey to become the best dad they can be and those who enjoy the spirit of motivation and competition to become the most incredible father of the year.

Let's elevate fatherhood together.

Part I

The Spark

      It was Valentine's Day weekend, and my wife had invited her college broommate, to visit. Every year after college, they would take turns visiting each other wherever they were. We had a small two-bedroom apartment, more so for the second closet rather than the second bed. The weekend was filled with gossip, catching up, and having a good time. I retired to the couch and teleported into Assassin's Creed: Black Flag. Annie had completed her Master's degree in Counseling Psychology and had secured a job working with sexually abused children. There was no shortage of information that they needed to catch up on.

I was trying to jumpstart my own practice after leaving my job as a high school counselor; however, the circumstances around my departure had never been fully communicated to anyone until now. The girls came up for air and required a third person to break the tie of which restaurant we would get chips and queso from; I happily obliged. After lunch, we temporarily enjoyed the sunny yet brisk temperatures before Annie's college roommate asked, "So what have you been up to?

This is where the drama begins.

I walked into work early and amped up because I had a great workout that morning. I usually arrive early, prioritize my tasks for the day, stand out in the halls, and welcome the students. This morning, however, several students came into my office with a similar concern.

"Mr. May, have you seen what's been happening on Twitter?" One asked me in a quiet and concerned tone. "I haven't," I admitted. I'd purposefully stayed away from Twitter because, at the beginning of the school, someone posted a picture of me standing outside my office with some "salacious captions." I valued my job and my freedom, so I never engaged.

"Two white female students recorded and released a song on SoundCloud and posted on Twitter! They say awful things about black people." I could see the look that said we're cool, but you're still an adult, and I'm not sure how you'd react if I said what I wanted to say.

"How about you just let me listen to it," I said nervously. One of the students closed the door and pressed play on their phone.

"N*ggas N*ggas N*ggas, they always look at me. I want to kill them; I want to hang them from a tree." My poker face is pretty good, but I was not expecting to hear that.

It's important to note that I am the only Black counselor in the entire district who served more than 13,000 students at a Title I school. I was also the only MALE counselor in the district. When the students brought this issue to my attention, the clip was already gaining traction with reporters and celebrities who had started to cover the story. There was no time for much besides trying to navigate the emotional rollercoaster of students, parents, and the community at large.

I spent the next 8 hours working through my own emotions while trying to discuss plans to deal with the powder keg of emotions within the school's leadership. When school let out that afternoon, I felt like I needed to make a response. Someone had to say something. Some had to acknowledge what had happened; someone had to teach these impressionable young minds what emotional intelligence is. To be angry, sad, disappointed, frustrated, and everything else in between and together. Too many marginalized people repress our gut instincts because we need to graduate, work, see them in the school pick-up line, at church, in our neighborhood, etc.

I am no stranger to small crowds or the spotlight, so I walked into the school's production studio, where the students learned how to make videos on a green screen, and made my response. It was one take. Raw, real, relevant. I spent a couple of hours at home editing the video, and then I posted it on YouTube and shared the link on Twitter on April 15.

The caption read:

I understand tempers are flaring, and people are opinionated at the moment. I feel that hurt and pain, but not just for myself, for what the ongoing ramifications will have on your lives and our world. I want the conversation of race to begin without polarizing individuals into two different camps. I hope it speaks to you and that, at our core, we can admit that we have a problem. We can show our support in different ways. I hope you will find a way to take a stand in a respectful manner and promote the conversation. #talkaboutit

When I woke up the following day, the video had garnered 2,000 views, around the same as the school's total student population. My office was filled to capacity when I arrived at work that day. There were calls for justice and vengeance, but more importantly, there was a sense of togetherness. Words cannot express how proud I was of all the students.

Later, on the second day of the SoundCloud incident, the students expected to hear a response from the school or the district. Unfortunately, I couldn't hide my disappointment regarding the lack of a prompt reply to condemn this behavior, even if it was delivered in the gentlest way possible.

I've never shared what happened next. On April 16, I floated the idea to a few of the students that if nothing happens, we'll stage a walkout. By now, Shaun King, an American writer and activist, along with Gabrielle Union, had actively made posts on social media about the rap song. I viewed it as a defining moment for many of our students. I let the carrier pigeons fly with the simple instructions.

Step 1. Pass the word out that those frustrated with this incident should wear all black on Thursday. I wanted to see it, and I wanted the students to find comfort in solidarity, but that was never going to be the end of it. The students and staff showed up in massive amounts, all black. We had the general support of the student body—I would say about one-third of the student body.

Step 2. Stage a sit-in/ Walk on Friday afternoon.
1. Record everything
2. Make signs

I worked with other staff members, including counselors, to organize places in the library where people could verbalize their frustrations on posters, murals, and other forms of expression.

It wasn't until Thursday afternoon that the district, in

combination with an apology from one of the girls, released a statement to the students and their families. Here is an expert from what I could find of that apology.

"I understand that there are many unanswered questions and multiple versions of rumors regarding when, where, and why the rap was made. I have never been so utterly humiliated and ashamed in my entire life because if you know me, you know you will never meet a human being with as much unconditional love and kindness in their heart as me.

First, I will address all questions regarding the specifics. I am currently a junior in high school and was a freshman at the time the song was recorded. It was a freestyle, meaning I just said whatever came to my head that would make people laugh. At this time in our lives, racism was not the talk of the country, nor had we ever witnessed the true power of social media; Twitter was still fresh, and we had never heard of anyone getting in trouble for posting anything on social media; it was the beginning of this social era. I was 14 years old and was ignorant of the words coming out of my mouth. As kids, we hear racist jokes at all times of the day. It's what we're around; it's the jokes we heard."

On Friday, April 17, tensions at the school were high, creating an atmosphere that felt like a powder keg ready to explode. As each minute passed without any incident, the day was deemed a success. The plan was for all students to leave the last lunch period and, after transitioning through the final two class periods—lasting 90 minutes—gather at the flagpole in front of the school.

Approximately 500 students exited the building but remained on campus, coming together in front of the school to listen, share, communicate, and express their feelings, mostly in a respectful manner. A week later, I announced that I would not be returning to my position as a counselor at the school.

Our visitor knew none of this drama. Her mouth stayed wide the entire time in disbelief as I shared the video footage from the walkout with her. (If you want to watch the initial response video and the montage from the walking out, visit Elevatefatherhood.com)
It was late afternoon, and the girls had to prepare for dinner. We went to our respective sides of the apartment for an "intensity" timeout. I plopped on the bed, exhausted yet energized at the same time. I vividly remember the following conversation. I'll look up at Annir from bed and notice the trail of clothes leading to the shower: "We'll both be busy with work this week, so if we don't have sex now, we probably won't until next weekend. Your friend is here, but we'll be quick and quiet." While talking, I stood up and walked over to the shower, turned it on, and then opened up both sink faucets and gave her that look. The look that says, you're gonna get it here, or in the shower you choose.

The experience from the walkout almost a year earlier had left a lasting impression. I needed to detox from the educational sphere altogether. However, I didn't have a consistent client base, and I substituted my income by driving from Uber. We foolishly believed that getting pregnant was going to be a long, arduous process, which meant that we weren't cautious at all. Annie's new job required her to be on staff for 3 months before her health benefits were activated, and we had run out of our supply of birth control. I can remember a single time when "mama flow" was a bit en retard. That's French for late. After a short but heroic performance, I popped out of the room, dressed, retook control of my throne, and continued to play Assassins Creed for the next hour until dinner.

Fast forward to six weeks later. March 11, 2016

We had just celebrated our 2nd year wedding anniversary the week before, and I was starting to look at other job opportunities. It was Friday morning, and I was lying on the bed with my back facing the long ensuite bathroom in our apartment. I was looking at my schedule for the day, and Annie was getting ready for work. Annie walked out of the bathroom, stood in the doorway, and casually said, "I think I missed my period this month."

A cold sweat started at my feet and slowly crawled up my spine. "Are you sure?" I asked, my voice a little too high-pitched to sound calm. My brain was racing as I turned around to peer into her eyes. What does "think" mean? How can you not be sure about something like that? But instead of saying any of that out loud, I just froze.

Within minutes, I was out the door, speeding to the nearest pharmacy, armed with a mission but absolutely zero preparation.

The pregnancy test aisle greeted me like a battle-field—a chaotic mess of pink and blue boxes, all claiming to be the best at detecting the "truth." There were at least ten different options, each more confusing than the last. Words like "early detection," "digital results," and "over 99% accurate" screamed at me from every box. And don't even get me started on the fine print. Did I need a regular test? A sensitive test? What about the one that claimed it could detect pregnancy up to six days earlier? Six days earlier than what?

I stood there meticulously re-reading labels and over-analyzing every word like I was preparing for a final exam. I picked up one box. "Clear results in under three minutes." Three minutes felt manageable—I mean, I could survive that amount of suspense. But then I saw another one that promised results in 60 seconds. Sixty seconds? That's a game-changer.

I can't help who I am, which is cheap. I wanted the faster test, but I also wanted the cheapest one. Why was one test $7 and another $27.99? Were the expensive ones better? Was the cheap one going to lie to me? I almost bought an ovulation test instead of a pregnancy test. I need to leave now.

After what felt like an eternity, I grabbed the cheapest test on the shelf, reasoning that they all had to be accurate if they were on the market. This was a rookie mistake. When I got home, I tossed the test onto the bed with a confidence I didn't feel.

"This'll do the trick," I said, sounding nonchalant. Annie stared at me, then at the generic-brand box, and back at me again, as if to say, Seriously? This is the best you could do?

I returned to the harsh fluorescent glow of a drugstore aisle and left with what can only be described as a cornucopia of pee sticks, desperately hoping at least one would tell a different story. Spoiler alert: they didn't. Every single test agreed—unanimously.

Annie was pregnant pregnant.

I teetered between pure panic and absolute elation. On the one hand, the math didn't add up: We didn't have great health insurance, I wasn't where I wanted to be in my career, Annie was three months into her first job as a therapist, we didn't own a house, and student loans loomed over us like dark clouds. What were we going to do?

Yet, at the same time, I was proud. Do you mean to tell me my "navy seal" swimmers evaded detection, out-maneuvered the enemy, flanked them, stormed the gates, and still managed to slip past the goalie? UNintentionally? I know that sounds insensitive to some, but at that moment, I felt like I had unlocked some kind of biological achievement.

Fatherhood is a gift and a choice, and I foolishly believed I was ready. I had no idea how wrong I was.

Setting the Framework

Before completing my undergraduate degree in theology, I had the opportunity to study in Greece and immerse myself in the world of ancient manuscripts and languages. One word stood out from my studies: telios. In Greek, telios embodies the idea of completeness or reaching one's ultimate purpose—not through perfection, but through progress and intentionality.

Fatherhood, much like telios, isn't about flawless execution; it's about showing up every day to create a meaningful legacy. Legacy isn't something we leave behind; it's something we cultivate daily—through our actions, reflections, and the systems we establish.

Legacy isn't something we leave behind; it's something we cultivate daily through our actions, reflections, and the systems we establish. But what does a system for building a legacy look like? How do we measure growth and progress in something as deeply personal as fatherhood? For centuries, humans have relied on frameworks—whether strategic plans, traditions, or guiding principles—to evaluate progress and make meaningful decisions.

Interestingly, woven into the fabric of key performance indicators is a narrative reflecting a father's determination to pass on his legacy to his adopted son. His approach to leadership and legacy demonstrates how intentional systems can shape personal outcomes and the futures of those we nurture.

Let's dive into the annals of history and uncover how an unassuming eunuch's wisdom laid the guiding principles of key performance indicators.

Let's begin where all great legacies start: with intention.

Lessons from Accient wisdom

The palace halls whispered with power, every stone echoing the stories of emperors, betrayals, and ambitions. In the heart of the Eastern Han dynasty, where fortunes could rise or fall with a single misstep, a eunuch named Cao Teng walked carefully but purposefully. His face bore the stillness of a man who understood that silence was often more powerful than words.

Cao Teng wasn't born into the world of courtly intrigue. He had once been a boy in a small farming village, a nameless child in the vastness of China. But fate had a cruel sense of humor. At a young age, his life took a brutal turn. Castration—a practice used to secure unquestionable loyalty to the imperial family—had robbed him of a future as a father or husband. However, it had opened doors to power he could never have imagined.

By the time he entered the palace, Cao Teng had already learned one of life's hardest lessons: survival depended on adaptation. And adapt he did. Cao Teng became a listener when others jostled for attention, shouting their loyalties and boasting of their virtues. He observed, learned, and positioned himself as the quiet, trustworthy presence the emperors desperately needed in their chaotic world.

It was the Emperor Huan who first truly saw Cao Teng's potential. While other advisors offered flattery, Cao

Teng provided wisdom. "Your enemies will not come at you with swords," he once told the emperor in a rare moment of candor. "They will come disguised as friends." The emperor had laughed at the time, but when a trusted ally betrayed him months later, Cao Teng remained by his side.

Through years of service, Cao Teng rose to become one of the most influential eunuchs of his era. His advice shaped policies, alliances, and, most importantly, succession plans. Choosing an heir was no small task—it was a decision that could ripple through generations, either stabilizing the empire or plunging it into chaos. Cao Teng's ability to evaluate character, loyalty, and ambition made him indispensable.

However, loyalty to the emperor did not mean loyalty to the imperial family. Cao Teng, for all his service, carried a secret dream—a hope that his name, his legacy, might live on despite his inability to have children. When the emperor allowed him to adopt a son, Cao Song, it was more than a privilege; it was the fulfillment of a profoundly personal ambition.

Cao Song was the perfect heir to carry on Cao Teng's name—obedient, mild-mannered, and eager to please. But it was his son, Cao Cao, who would become the true embodiment of Cao Teng's legacy.

From the moment he was born, Cao Cao was different. As a child, he was restless, clever, and prone to mischief. He would often sneak into the palace archives, pouring over military strategies and poetry with equal fervor. His grand-father's reputation granted him access to the imperial court, where he observed the political machinations of the Han dynasty firsthand.

But Cao Cao was not content with being a specta-tor. He dreamed of greatness—not the kind earned through titles and formalities, but the kind etched into the annals of history. While others saw the fractured state of China as a tragedy, Cao Cao saw it as an opportunity. He believed that the chaos of the warring states could be turned into order, but only under the rule of someone strong enough, cunning enough, to unite them. And he was sure that person was himself.

By the time he reached adulthood, Cao Cao had de-veloped a reputation as both a military genius and a deeply complicated man. His strategies on the battlefield were un-matched. At the Battle of Guandu, faced with a vastly larger army under Yuan Shao, Cao Cao used deception, sabotage, and superior tactics to secure a victory that would cement his dominance in northern China. It was the kind of brilliance that made his allies cheer and his enemies shudder.

But Cao Cao was not without his flaws. He was par-anoid to a fault, often suspecting betrayal even where there was none. His cruelty was infamous—entire villages were burned in his campaigns, their ashes serving as grim remind-ers of his ruthlessness. Yet, there was another side to him, one that baffled even his closest advisors. Late at night, after battles had been fought and decisions made, Cao Cao would retreat to his tent and compose poetry.

In one of his most famous poems, he wrote:

"Facing the tide, I think of the heroes of old.
My heart aches for their wisdom.
The waves crash and retreat—
Each generation leaves its mark,
Only for the sands to reclaim it."

Cao Cao was a man torn between ambition and reflection, between the pursuit of power and the quiet understanding of its impermanence.

Through all his victories and defeats, Cao Cao never forgot the influence of his grandfather. He often spoke of the systems Cao Teng had put in place—the evaluations of character, the foresight in planning—that had given him his start in life. "Without him," Cao Cao once said, "I would have been another forgotten soul in a time of chaos."

Cao Teng's wisdom not only shaped emperors but also prepared Cao Cao for the challenges of leadership. Even after Cao Teng's death, his legacy lived on in the way Cao Cao measured progress—not just in battles won but in the loyalty he inspired and the future he built.

In his later years, when Cao Cao established the Cao Wei state, he posthumously honored Cao Teng as the first emperor of Wei. This tribute was not just to a man but to the ideals he embodied: strategy, reflection, and the courage to and purpose.

While Cao Cao's ambitions were measured in battles and political alliances, his legacy reminds us of a simple truth: success, whether in leadership, business, or life, thrives on reflection and intentional action. And just like in the days of ancient China, today we rely on systems like KPIs to give us that clarity—to evaluate where we are, where we're going, and how we can improve along the way."

Pause & Reflect

Cao Teng, despite his limitations, built a legacy through intentional actions and systems. What small, consistent actions are you taking today that could leave a lasting impact on your children or community?

How Do You Measure Progress in Fatherhood?
Cao Teng and Cao Cao relied on systems to navigate chaos and make critical decisions. If you were to define "success" in your role as a father, what personal Key Performance Indicators (KPIs) would you track?

guide others toward greatness.

Cao Cao's story contains contradictions—ruthlessness and kindness, ambition and doubt, brilliance and paranoia. He saw the cracks in the world and tried to mend them, even if it meant breaking a few pieces along the way. And yet, for all his power and influence, his legacy was built on the foundation laid by his grandfather.
Cao Teng, the eunuch who could never father a child, became the grandfather of one of China's greatest warlords. His quiet, unassuming wisdom was the force that shaped an empire.

And perhaps that is the greatest lesson of their story: that true legacy isn't always loud. Sometimes, it's the quiet influence, the unseen guidance, that leaves the most lasting mark.

If you've ever worked in an environment where performance evaluations are the norm, you already have more in common with Cao Cao than you might think. The story of Cao Teng and Cao Cao is a powerful testament to the importance of systems, intentionality, and foresight.

Cao Teng didn't leave success to luck or instinct—he created a framework to evaluate performance, assess character, and guide crucial decisions. These systems didn't guarantee flawless outcomes, but they brought clarity in moments of uncertainty, enabling him—and later, his grandson, Cao Cao—to navigate the chaos of their time with precision

How Do You Balance Ambition and Reflection?
Like Cao Cao, fathers often juggle the drive to achieve with the need to reflect. Are you creating space to pause, evaluate your actions, and recalibrate to ensure your ambitions align with the legacy you want to leave?

Key Performace Indicators Explained

Today, we call those systems Key Performance Indicators, or KPIs. While the stakes may not always involve dynasties or empires, the principles remain the same.

A KPI is a measurable value that shows how effectively a

person, organization, or business is achieving its goals. It's a tool that helps us focus on what matters, track progress, and adjust our approach as needed.

Just as Cao Teng used evaluation systems to guide emperors and ensure stability, KPIs are modern tools for measuring success in our endeavors. They provide a framework for reflection and accountability, enabling us to grow, improve, and make informed decisions in real-time. But KPIs aren't just for businesses or governments. Imagine if you could apply the same concept to your personal life, your relationships, or even your role as a parent.

What would your Key Performance Indicators of fatherhood look like? How would you measure progress in something as complex and deeply personal as raising a child?

KPIs aren't about perfection—they're about progress. They remind us that growth isn't linear and success isn't always immediate. Having a clear vision of where you want to go and the willingness to reflect and adjust along the way matters

.

Let's examine KPIs, why they matter, and how they can help us in areas as diverse as business, personal development, and parenting. Whether you're running an empire or a household, clarity and reflection are the keys to meaningful progress.

How would you measure success in something as

complex and deeply personal as raising a child? Fatherhood doesn't come with a user manual, but it does come with moments—big and small—that show us how we're doing. Whether it's the way your child runs into your arms at the end of a long day or the laughter you share over bedtime stories, these moments are clues. They're the building blocks of what truly matters.

KPIs aren't about perfection—they're about progress. They remind us that growth isn't linear and success isn't always immediate. They're not rigid rules to follow but tools to reflect on how far we've come and where we want to go. In fatherhood, these indicators go beyond milestones or achievements. They reflect the heart of parenting—your love, your presence, and your commitment to nurturing a well-rounded, emotionally healthy, and confident child.

In many ways, KPIs of fatherhood are personal benchmarks. They're not just about what you do; they're about how you show up. Are you listening when your child needs you? Are you patient when it's hard? Are you creating moments that your child will carry with them for the rest of their lives?

Before we dive deeper into the journey of fatherhood, take a moment to pause and reflect. Picture the father you are today. Is he the dad who reads every night before bed? The dad who makes pancakes on Saturday mornings? Now, think about the father you want to become. Is he the one who balances work and family with grace? The one who

builds traditions, inspires resilience, and leaves a legacy of
lov

Pause & Reflect

Fatherhood isn't about assigning yourself a grade or meeting impossible standards. It's about showing up, learning, and growing. Reflection is where it all begins. Take a deep breath, and let these questions guide you inward. The father you are today is just the story's first chapter—the best is yet to come.

How do you, if at all, measure progress in your fatherhood journey?

Reflect on your actions and decisions as a father over the past three months. Can you pinpoint a moment where you acted with clear purpose or intentionality to guide, support, or inspire your child? Write down that example and consider how it aligns with the father you aspire to be.

Pregnancy Confirmed

The first lesson fatherhood teaches you is that you're not in control. We had to wait a week before seeing an OBGYN to confirm the pregnancy. My mom told me that "wait training" is the most complex and challenging training for building your patience muscles.

In the meantime, we had big decisions, such as which OBGYN to use. Annie and I have always made significant decisions together. However, as a biracial couple, cultural considerations added another layer of complexity. Annie spent hours reading Google reviews before finally booking an appointment.

Meanwhile, I spent that week talking crazy with a capital C. "Wouldn't it be wild if we had twins?" And then, "I had a dream we're having a boy and a girl." Annie alternated between rolling her eyes and ignoring me, but the tension between us kept building as the appointment drew closer.

Wednesday, March 23, 2016

The day of the appointment finally arrived. We pulled up to the hospital complex, both nervous but showing it in different ways. My default setting is Excited. Annie is anxious. It was game day, jitters. While waiting for the elevator, I kissed her forehead before heading inside; she grabbed my shoulder and said, "Don't be weird." I locked eyes with her, smiled warmly, and squeezed her hand. Then, taking a deep breath, I said, "Game time," followed by a DMX-style growl.

Listen to We Ready by Archie Eversole if you want to get in the same headspace. "You're welcome."

We headed up to the third floor, where Annie checked in while I wandered over to the wall of employee photos. I was already practicing my dad's pose, hands on hips, feet shoulder apart, acting as a building inspector. He seemed like the perfect combination of confident, capable, and caring.

When the nurse called us back for the ultrasound, I couldn't stop talking. I commented on the layout, cracked jokes, and made random observations as if my nervous energy was going to be on display. That is until Annie crushed my hand with a bone-crunching grip.

Dr. Branning walked in with a warm smile that immediately helped ease some of the tension. "Don't worry," he said, sensing our nerves. "I've already seen nine sets of twins this year, so I think we've hit our quota."

"Nine?" I joked, leaning back in the chair. "You can't end on an odd number, Doc. That's just bad luck."

The room chuckled—well, most of the room. Annie didn't seem amused.

Dr. Branning smirked as he adjusted the ultrasound machine. "Alright, let's see what's going on here," he said, slipping into his professional demeanor.

The room quieted, the hum of the machine filling the air as the wand glided across Annie's belly. I was leaning forward now, my eyes fixed on the screen, watching shadows and shapes I couldn't quite make out. Annie stayed focused on the ceiling. Her hands clasped over her stomach until she felt an announcement coming."You're definitely pregnant, with twins," he said with a gasp. He moved the ultrasound wand and let us listen to the heartbeats.

"Come again?" my brain said. The room suddenly felt too small; perhaps I should have listened and sat down. Annie looked ghostly pale, her face a mix of fear and shock, while her eyes were conveying communication: "You did this to me."

"And," the doctor started up again, "I'm hearing a third heartbeat, which could be an echo of the exterior wall because

I can't see the third baby. It does sound like a distinct third heartbeat."

I let out a quieter scream, considering my level of excitement. For a brief moment, I was transported to a locker full of players spraying champagne because we won the championship. Spontaneous triplets. No IVF, no fertility treatments—this was an achievement most people wouldn't believe. My "navy seals" had pulled off a biological miracle. I felt like the Michael Jordon of reproduction.

But that moment of celebration didn't last long. It was like someone pulled the fire alarm in the middle of my imag-inary locker room celebration, leaving me standing there, drenched in sweat, holding a champagne bottle I had no idea what to do with.

Reality hit hard.

My mind started racing with every worry I'd been holding back. Three babies? At the same time? I wasn't wor-ried about being a dad—I had always wanted kids. But three at once? That's a whole squad. I barely knew how to take care of myself some days. Who was going to take care of these three tiny humans?

We don't even have a house big enough for this. My brain threw logistical concerns at me like dodgeballs. Where are we going to fit three cribs? What about a car big enough for car seats? Do strollers even come in triplet models?

And then the financial panic set in. How much do diapers

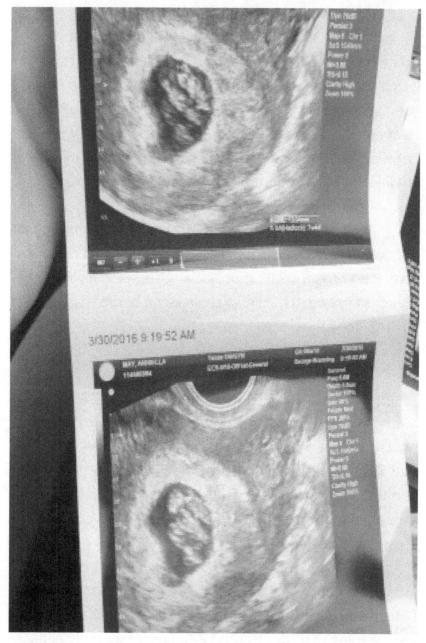

is messy and unpredictable, but it's also incredible.
In my head, the champagne celebration started again. This
time, it wasn't about the achievement. It was about the gift.

"I'll need to see you back next week to confirm, but
you guys would be my first triplet pregnancy this year." Dr.
Branning said with a large smile. " I know I just met you, but
you seem like this is something the two of you can handle."

It's the greatest lifelong challenge I could have asked for.

Before we left Dr. Branning's office, he scheduled
us for an appointment with a maternal-fetal specialist and
wished us well. He explained that maternal-fetal specialists
handle complex pregnancies—the kinds that not only make
textbooks but also rewrite them.

I mean, come on. Spontaneous triplets. What were the odds? No treatments, no medical interventions—just a one-in-10,000 chance. This wasn't just biology. It felt like fate, like I was meant to be their dad. It was as if the universe had looked at me and Annie and said, You two can handle this. You've got this.

Suddenly, the things I was worried about didn't seem as important. We would figure out the logistics. The diapers. The strollers. The house. We'd find a way to make it work. I went to high school with triplet girls, and if they could do it, so could we. The weight of responsibility was still there, but so was the realization that I wasn't doing this alone. Annie and I were a team. We'd been through challenges before, and we'd face this one together. I started to think about the joy, the chaos, the love that was about to enter our lives. Three babies.

I went from drowning in worry to feeling like I was about to embark on the adventure of a lifetime. I pictured the laughter and the milestones—the first steps, the first words, the late-night feeding marathons that would drive us crazy but also bring us closer together.

I looked at Annie, who was still in shock, and gave her hand a reassuring squeeze. "Three babies," I whispered, more to myself than to her. A smile crept across my face. Three little miracles.
Sure, we weren't remotely prepared. But whois? Fatherhood

Part II

The Forge

Wednesday, March 23, 2016

I couldn't push the elevator button fast enough.

The ride down to the ground floor was silent. Neither of us said a word, but the tension between us was electric, like a wire pulled taut. I glanced at Annie, whose face looked flat—like she was suppressing excitement, terror, or a combination of both. I wasn't sure what to say, so I stayed quiet, holding on to her.

As soon as the doors slid open, Annie was on her phone.

¡Hola?!" my mother-in-law, Monica, answered, her voice filled with nervous excitement that practically crackled through the phone. Monica and Osvaldo, my in-laws, are Argentinian immigrants who came to the U.S. A country girl from a small town with a big personality, Monica still works as a nurse today, and even after decades in America, her accent hasn't faded a bit.

This was their first grandbaby, and Monica's excitement was on a level I hadn't fully appreciated until that moment. If joy had a volume setting, Monica's was cranked to max.

"Is Papi there?" Annie asked quickly, her voice shaking just enough to betray the whirlwind of emotions she was holding back.

"¿Sí? Why? How did it go?" Monica's words tumbled out like a waterfall, spilling over one another in her eagerness to know.

We waited a few moments for Osvaldo to join the call. In the background, I could hear his beloved rocking chair creak as he stood up and shuffled closer to the phone.

"Well," Annie started, "we're definitely pregnant..."

Monica gasped audibly, but before she could say anything, Annie continued.

"... and we're having twins."

The "S" on "twins" was barely out of her mouth before I broke my silence. "No, TRIPLETS!" I yelled loud enough to echo off the walls of the parking garage.

The phone went silent for a beat as if the words needed a moment to settle. "There was a chorus of "No, no, no, how, No?" followed by "Para de jorobar, che!" (Stop playing around). My in-laws argued over whether we were joking before finally exploding with laughter, disbelief, and something resembling relief that they were going to be grandparents.

"¡Wow! You were right, Marland," Monica said, "About having twins," she chuckled.

Before I could ask what exactly she meant by "you were right," Annie smacked me on the arm. I can't remember much else from that moment because I'm pretty confident she hit me so many times she gave me a mild concussion. But I do vaguely remember Osvaldo chuckling in the background, muttering about how we'd better start buying diapers in bulk.

The call to my parents was far less dramatic, though no less memorable. My parents, who will celebrate their 50th wedding anniversary in April 2025, are in their late 70s and 80s. I'm the 3rd child of four boys, with my older brother already married with two kids and my younger brother yet to start family planning. My parents had been through two grandkid births already, but this news? This was something entirely new.

I called my mom first. I could hear my dad's voice in the background, and I waited until he was within earshot before delivering the news.

"What's the word, son?" my dad called out in his usual chipper tone. "Well," I said, trying to sound as calm as possible, "we're definitely pregnant. It's twins for sure, and there's a high likelihood it's triplets."

My mom gasped, and the line went dead for half a second before a series of chuckles and wows filled the void.

"WOW! Oh my God! Lord Jesus, what a miracle, oh gosh, but—how?!" She tumbled through her exclamations, each one more dramatic than the last. I didn't have to see her to know she'd already clasped her hands to her chest, her mind racing between disbelief and pure joy.

My dad, on the other hand, was taking it all in stride. I could picture his face exactly: the exaggerated expressions, the big grin that showed his overlapping bottom teeth, and that deep, booming laugh that always came from his gut. "Well, well," he chuckled. God is good. Let's get these out so we can get three more!"

We didn't talk long. Annie and I were running on fumes and needed to get home, but those conversations stayed with me. Sharing the news felt good, but it also brought a quiet sense of finality: this was real now.

"Silence is golden." That was the old AMC slogan, but it also became the unspoken rule of how we lived for the next week. Annie's birthday was the next day, and there was no way we would keep a lid on this secret. Between family gatherings and the fact that neither of our parents could hold water when it came to big news, I was positive the WhatsApp messages were already flying back and forth around the globe.

But the real issue—the one that weighed heavily on my mind—was the potential for loss.

Several years earlier, my closest friend, mentor, and wife had experienced the unimaginable. Their child was stillborn due to complications, and though I had heard the story from their lips, it was somehow even more haunting to listen to it from the doctor who had delivered the baby. My mentor and his wife, two of the strongest, most faith-filled people I know, belted Christian hymns through every push, every gut-wrenching moment, knowing they would meet their child lifeless in the end. It wasn't a story you just hear and forget. It lingers like a shadow and emerges in the moments you least expect.
That memory haunted every waking moment of the week ahead. Every time I allowed myself to feel even a shred of joy about the possibility of triplets, the fear of that potential reality pulled me back down.

We hobbled through the rest of the week like zombies, full of love, fear, and just enough hope to keep moving forward.

At some point, the excitement of what could be started to push the fear aside. After all, we were pregnant—pregnant! That fact alone deserved celebration. As cheesy as I know this sounds, I always hoped I'd discover I would be a dad through some kind of cutesy surprise. You know, like one of those Pinterest-worthy announcements with a riddle or a box of tiny Baby Jordans sitting next to a fresh pair of Jordans for me. I'd pick up the box, put two and two together, and then cry tears of joy while Annie recorded it on her phone.

That wasn't how things went down, obviously. Instead, we found ourselves scrambling to put together our "announcement," trying to channel that Pinterest energy with whatever we had. Before heading to the store, we grabbed an empty box and scribbled a quick note to let my brother and sister-in-law know they were about to become an aunt and uncle. It wasn't elegant or exceptionally well-planned, but it would have to do.

Annie's birthday falls the day after my brother and sister-in-law's wedding anniversary, and in our families, the slightest hint of a special occasion is all the excuse anyone needs to gather everyone and anyone for an impromptu celebration.

We headed out to the restaurant on a cold and rainy night. The air outside was crisp, but inside the restaurant, it was chaotic—dimly lit, packed with people, and so loud we practically had to yell just to place our orders. It was also the first time we'd seen my in-laws since breaking the news about potentially having triplets, and their excitement was radiating off of them like heat.

When the moment came, Annie and I handed my brother and sister-in-law the box. "We have a surprise for you," I said, shoving it into their hands and awkwardly lingering until they started to open it. The box sat in their laps for a second, the dim lighting making it hard to read the note. For a moment, I thought the announcement might flop. But then, my sister-in-law's jaw literally dropped, her expression morphing from confusion to shock to joy and round and round.

"You're pregnant?" she gasped.
"Yup," Annie said with a grin.
"Congratulations?" my brother-in-law said.
"With TWINS?!" My sister-in-law said
"Yes, and potentially triplets."

The table erupted. Gasps, laughter, and a few "Are you serious?!" responses reverberated through the restaurant. Our little announcement had landed.

We invited some of Annie's closest friends to my brother-in-law's house a few nights later. The weather had cleared up, but the air was still cool, and the house was small enough to make the gathering feel intimate.

As soon as they arrived, we started giving them a

"tour" of the house, mainly to get everyone into one room so we could announce the news. Unsurprisingly, the tour was over in about 90 seconds. The house wasn't exactly a sprawling estate, and the tension of keeping our secret made us eager to skip to the main event.

Before we could say anything, Annie's close friend— blurted out, "I'm getting strong pregnancy vibes from some- one in this room."
We froze.

Annie's friend, who was deep into what was proba- bly her third glass of wine, narrowed her eyes and scanned the room. "You guys know I'm psychic, right?" she said with a smirk. We all laughed, though the nervous laughter came when someone was a little too close to the truth.

"I'm pregnant," Annie said, her voice cutting through the ten- sion like a knife. Gasps filled the room, followed by a chorus of congratulations. The excitement was palpable, but Annie wasn't finished.

"But not with just one baby," she added quickly.

"Twins?!" someone shouted, their voice tinged with joy and disbelief.
"Potentially triplets," Annie said, barely getting the words out before the chorus of "WTFs" began.

The room erupted into chaos again, with everyone

talking at once, trying to process what they'd just heard. For a moment, it was overwhelming—but in the best possible way.

Unbearable News

April 1, 2016

It was time to call Annie's college roommate and explain how her presence stimulated our genetic material enough to conceive, replicate, and duplicate miraculously. We were going on a family camping trip, so we FaceTimed her in the car. Annie confirmed that we were pregnant and continued,I'm not just pregnant with one baby. Robin's eyes grow big, and her mouth opens.

"And I'm not just pregnant with two babies," Annie said, watching her friend's face twist in confusion. Are you having a dog?" a confused Robin asked.

"No, "Annie says with a nervous chuckle. We're pregnant with triplets." Shock, happiness, confusion, laughter, joy, and questions exist as expected.

We got off the phone pretty quickly after that statement and tried to soak in nature. The trees, the water, the wind, and the cool air offered a brief reprieve before the reality of seeing the specialist a few days later loomed large in our minds.

But even amidst the uncertainty, life doesn't pause. There were people to share the news with—people who had unknowingly contributed to this miraculous journey. The week before meeting with Dr. Stewart, the maternal-fetal medicine specialist, had been a rollercoaster of emotions, and we still had no guarantees about what was to come. But for now, we held onto the joy. We laughed with family and friends and dreamed about life with three babies.

Sometimes, the only way to cope with uncertainty is to embrace the moments of joy when they come.

Tuesday, April 19, 2016

It had been exactly three weeks since we confirmed our pregnancy, and today was the day—the appointment with our maternal- fetal medicine specialist, Dr. Stewart. The air in the car was thick with unspoken emotions as we drove 5 minutes to the hospital complex. It was a prominent, imposing place, almost overwhelming in size, but somehow, we found the tiny office tucked away in a corner of one of the towering buildings.

When we walked in, we were greeted by warm, friendly faces— faces that immediately felt comforting. The staff here wasn't just knowledgeable; experts in navigating high-risk pregnancies' stress and uncertainty. Their familiarity with this world softened some of the anxiety that had been building inside me all week.

Ironically, as rare as triplets are, we weren't the only triplet parents in the waiting room. This wasn't their first rodeo, which was strangely reassuring. The nurse assigned to our case, a woman who radiated kindness, casually mentioned that she was the mother of 12-year-old triplets—two girls and a boy. She shared this as if it were the most ordinary thing in the world, but to us, it felt like meeting someone from an exclusive club.

As she checked Annie's vitals—height, weight, blood pressure—it became abundantly clear that she was very pregnant. The increased weight gain, elevated blood pressure, and morning sickness weren't just signs anymore; they were undeniable evidence of the three tiny lives growing inside her.

The nurse continued to share her experiences as a triplet mom while leading us back to the ultrasound room. Hearing her talk was uniquely comforting. When you're part of such a rare and elite group, an unspoken connection forms—a bond forged in shared understanding.

Because the truth is, not everyone gets it. People can empathize, sure. They can nod and offer kind words. But only someone who's been through it knows the reality of carrying, delivering, and raising three babies at once. The stress, the fear, the endless unknowns—it's a language only other triplet parents speak fluently.

And in that moment, we just needed someone who understood. Annie climbed onto the medical table, the paper cover crinkling beneath her as she rolled up her shirt. She shivered slightly when the ultrasound gel hit her belly, the coldness pulling her out of her thoughts for a moment. She looked at me and mouthed, "Don't be weird."

Well, that was easier said than done.

By now, I was convinced I was an expert in reading the striations and shadows on the ultrasound screen. I'd seen enough YouTube videos, sat through enough late-night Googling sessions, and listened to enough medical explanations to think I could tell a hand from a foot or a heartbeat from a glitch. Of course, I couldn't tell anything apart—but that didn't stop me from staring intently, pretending I could. I engaged in light chatter with the ultrasound tech to distract myself from the nerves bubbling beneath the surface. It was easier to ask casual questions about her weekend than to think too hard about what we might see on the screen. But mostly, I wanted her to just tell me so that we wouldn't have to wait longer for answers.

And then I felt it—a sharp, searing pain in my fingers. Annie was gripping my hand, her knuckles white, her grip strong enough to rival an Olympic weightlifter's. My knuckles crunched under the pressure. No one had warned me that pregnancy came with increased strength, but apparently, that was a thing.

I looked over at her, but her eyes were glued to the screen. She was holding my hand as a precaution—to keep me from being "weird." Unfortunately for me, that also meant keeping me silent. I got the message.
I remained mute for the rest of the ultrasound, my hand throbbing as a reminder to behave myself.

The room was dimly lit, with the only light coming from the glowing screen as the tech carefully moved the ultrasound wand across Annie's belly. Her voice was calm and steady, and she explained measurements and landmarks as she worked. I nodded along, pretending to understand, but my mind was racing.

While we waited for Dr. Stewart to arrive, I reached for my phone and started recording. I figured it was harmless—just some footage to document the experience, maybe even share with family later. But looking back, that video became more than just a memory.

It became a lifeline.

What happened next was traumatic in a way that words fail to capture. Even now, as I sit here writing this, I find that specific details are locked away, buried deep in the recesses of my subconscious where I can't—or won't—access them. It's as if my brain decided that remembering them too vividly would hurt too much.

I've had to revisit that footage just to piece this chapter together, to remind myself of what we saw, what we heard, and what we felt in those moments.
Because in that room, everything changed.

A soft tapping at the door broke the silence, followed by the slow creak of heavy, weighted medical doors swinging open. The room was dim, the glow from the ultrasound screen our only light source, until the brightness of the outside corridor spilled in, momentarily blinding us.
And there he was.

Standing in the doorway was Dr. Stewart, a five-foot-nine man with dark brown hair and a neatly trimmed beard, dressed in a crisp collared shirt with a standard-issued white coat. He had a calm presence about him, almost like a figure from a religious painting, though the resemblance didn't bring me much comfort at that moment. Maybe it was because no matter who walked through that door—doctor, saint, or miracle worker—they couldn't change what this moment might mean.

He stepped into the room, introduced himself with a warm smile, and extended his hand. His handshake was firm but not overbearing, and as he sat down, I noticed his movements were deliberately grounded. He carried himself like someone who had done this a thousand times but still understood that it was the first for us.

I can't tell you much of what he said in the moments that followed. His words escaped me almost as soon as they left his lips. But what I can tell you is that his presence was steadying—like a lighthouse in a storm. He spoke with a calm precision that told us he wouldn't sugarcoat anything. He was straightforward, transparent, and honest. At that moment, that was exactly what we needed.

Dr. Stewart rolled his chair closer to us. His demeanor remained calm and measured, but there was something in his eyes, a heaviness, that hinted at the conversation we were about to have.

It was time for that talk.

"The type of pregnancy you've been blessed with," he began, "is in the top 1% of the highest-risk pregnancies there is. It's called Monochorionic Monoamnionnic Triplets." He paused, giving the words space to land.

"The probability of this type of pregnancy," he continued, "is one in maybe 120,000 to a million type of pregnancies. This occurring naturally is even lower, all three babies making its term even lower. "

I leaned back in my chair, sensing his words press against my chest. One in a million. I let that phrase echo in my mind for a moment, somewhere between awe and fear.

Dr. Stewart adjusted his tone, speaking carefully but clearly, like a teacher explaining a complex concept to a student. "What this means," he said, "is that you have an identical set of twins and a singleton triplet. In the case of the twins, there's no dividing wall between them. Let me explain this in layman's terms: Imagine a house. In a normal house, all of the dangerous components—electrical wiring, heating, plumbing—are safely enclosed in separate rooms. But in an open- concept house, everything merges together. There's no separation, and it's easier for things to tangle, overlap, or malfunction."

He glanced at Annie, then at me, pausing to ensure we understood. "This is an open-concept situation inside Annie's womb. And in this unfinished environment, the probability of cords and other dangerous factors impacting one or both of the twins is high. Not just high—very high."
The room was silent except for the faint hum of machinery. I gripped Annie's hand tightly, feeling the cold sweat on my palms and wondering if she could feel it, too.

"Baby A," he began, "has developed a large mass at the base of her skull. Her intestines are also abnormally large and are not retreating into her belly button as they should be at this stage."

The words hung in the air, heavy and suffocating. "This could indicate severe deformities, physical challenges, or other health complications—if she survives," he continued. Annie's grip on my hand tightened, and I felt her nails dig into my skin.

"Babies B and C," Dr. Stewart went on, "are in extremely tight quarters. If the umbilical cords get tangled, circulating dangerously close to them. There's a high probability that one or both may not survive."

He took a deep breath before laying out our options: Selective reduction: We could reduce one of the twins to improve the survival chances of the other two. Monitoring Baby A: We could continue to monitor her development to determine the potential challenges she might face if she survived, knowing this would add immense difficulty to raising twins alongside a child with severe disabilities.

Do nothing: We could continue the pregnancy as it was, knowing that we might lose one, two, or all three babies.

"There's also a possibility," he added, "that the body may absorb one of the babies B and C, which could result in reducing risk and increasing odds of survival. I sat there, stunned, trying to process the fact that the appointment was only 30 minutes long—and we'd already been there for 25. How were we supposed to make sense of the next chapter of our lives in five minutes?

I tend to find safety in numbers and facts. When emotions run high, I anchor myself in probabilities, percentages, and data points. They help me think clearly, cut through the noise, and make decisions with purpose. So, sitting across from Dr. Stewart, trying to process the overwhelming weight of the moment, I clung to that instinct. I needed the numbers. I needed the facts.

"What are our odds?" I asked, breaking the silence. "What are the chances? What are the facts?" I observed his face, scanning his eyes for any flicker, any twitch, anything that might reveal what he really thought. His poker face was solid—too solid. He exhaled slowly as though the weight of his answer might crush the room. "There's a 60% chance you could lose all of them," he said evenly.

The words hung in the air, suspended like lead balloons. Sixty percent. Not fifty. It's not a coin toss. It wasn't hope—it was survival odds.

If you've been in boardrooms or played sports, this should feel familiar. Don't get excited, and don't lose focus; breathe and execute the plan, but stay nimble. Dr. Stewart's voice didn't waver as he continued. "You should prepare yourselves for the possibility of making difficult choices in the weeks ahead. This pregnancy, while miraculous, carries significant risks. We could lose one of the twins and have the fraternal triplet. We could lose both twins and only have the fraternal. We could lose all three. You could give birth to three stillborn babies."

He paused again, letting the words hang in the air. My stomach tightened as its gravity began to sink in.
"There's also a possibility," he added, "that the body may absorb one or more of the babies, which could create complications later in the pregnancy. For now, we'll monitor you weekly to track the babies' progress. As of today, there are no restrictions on your movements or lifestyle, but if anything unusual happens, please contact my office immediately."

Annie nodded mechanically as though her body had gone on autopilot. I glanced at her, searching her face for any hint of what she was feeling, but all I could see was the faint trembling of her lips. I felt the enormity of the moment, the weight of all the outcomes

Dr. Stewart had laid before us. It was as if we had been handed a delicate treasure—a one-in-a-million miracle—but told it could shatter at any moment.

Fear meets Faith

As Dr. Stewart walked us out of the room, his words still swirling in my mind, I found myself clinging to something more profound than logic. We're pregnant with a rare case of triplets, I thought. This wasn't some random coincidence; it felt ordained, designed, and written into the fabric of our lives long before we even entered the picture. Surely, I reasoned, a divine creator wouldn't bless us with something this rare, this extraordinary, only to rip it away in the most painful way imaginable. Indeed, this miracle was meant to be.

But faith can be tricky when mixed with fear. The two can coexist, pulling you in opposite directions and leaving you suspended between hope and heartbreak.
I squeezed Annie's hand as we walked down the long corridor. She was silent, her footsteps light and deliberate, as if she were trying to carry the weight of the world as gracefully as possible. I leaned over and whispered in her ear.

"Isn't this great news? We've just hit the lottery," I said with a slight chuckle, hoping to lighten the moment. She didn't respond, her eyes fixed on the ground ahead of us. As we walked out of the hospital, the late afternoon sunlight bathed the parking lot, cutting through the tension that had followed us all morning. For a moment, I let myself imagine a future that wasn't shrouded in uncertainty. I pictured us holding three tiny bundles of joy, hearing three sets of cries, and feeling the chaotic beauty of a life we had only begun to grasp. For now, though, there was nothing else to do but take a deep breath, hold Annie's hand, and keep walking forward.

Despite all this excitement, life was moving forward in unexpected ways. My parents were in the process of downsizing from the house I had grown up in. The house that shaped me.

My dad, always a planner, had been preparing for this phase of life for as long as I could remember. As a much older father compared to my friends' dads, he had spent years talking about inheritance, legacy, and the practicalities of aging. So when I'd told him about the triplets—about our fears, about how we weren't sure how we would make it all work—he made an offer. "How about you and your wife move into this house?" he said matter-of-factly. "It's already set up for a family of five. Your mother and I will move into the other property, just thirty minutes away."

I froze.

I'm not someone who takes handouts easily. I have a hard time accepting anything I don't feel like I've earned. But I also knew my dad, a man who had spent his life making sacrifices for his family, wasn't offering this lightly. This was part of his plan. Still, the house wasn't just a home—it was a symbol. Let me explain.

On my seventh birthday, my parents told me and my brothers that we were moving from Oklahoma to Paris, France. My dad, who worked for American Airlines' technology division, known as Sabre and later on EDS, had been offered a once-in-a-lifetime opportunity: to provide tech support for the French National Transit System, the SNCF.

For five years, we lived abroad, immersed in a world where we didn't speak the language but had the most incredible experiences. My worldview, my perspective, the foundation of who I am today—all of it was shaped during that time.

When we returned to the States in the summer of 1995, our family purchased a home, the Burbs, because we had grown accustomed to the tranquility of the countryside. My older brother was due to start high school in a year, and we were all settling in for our family's next adventure.

On my dad's side of the family, we have a natural athletic gift. I was a promising young athlete—a six-foot 2 inch, overgrown 14-year-old who'd been elected varsity captain of the football team. The opportunities in front of me were immense and could have rewritten my future entirely. But we were a family of faith. We honored the Jewish Sabbath, and Friday night football games clashed with our traditions. At 16, I made the decision to walk away from football. It wasn't an easy choice, but it was the right one for me. That house became a place where I wrestled with dreams and discipline, ambition and values. Now, years later, I found myself returning to it—not as a teenager but as a soon-to-be father of three.

The house held memories and ghosts, but it also offered us the space and stability we desperately needed. So we moved in between week 10 and week 13, planting roots in the same place where I'd grown.

Reflect. Recalibrate. Refine.

Moving into my childhood home wasn't just a logistical decision; it was a moment of reflection and reckoning. It forced me to confront my past—the values instilled in me, the choices I made, and the ways my parents supported and guided me through their quiet actions. My father's willingness to offer the home wasn't just a practical solution; it was a profound symbol of the systems he had put in place to keep our family rooted and aligned.

That house wasn't just a structure of wood and brick. It was an architectural framework of memories, values, and intentional support—a design my parents had built, consciously or not, to ensure we thrived. It made me realize that fatherhood requires more than showing up; it demands a blueprint for how we provide, adapt, and respond to the needs of those who depend on us.

Living there again, as an adult and a soon-to-be father of triplets, I saw how essential it was to build my own framework. I thought about how my parents had always been attuned to our needs, adjusting their approach as life evolved. My dad's decision to offer us the home wasn't just a gesture of generosity; it was an act of intentional support, a reinforcement of the foundation they had built for our family.

It became clear to me that feedback—both given and received— is the cornerstone of that foundation. Fatherhood isn't about rigidly sticking to a plan; it's about creating a dynamic system that allows for reflection, recalibration, and growth. Just as children grow and change, so must the way we show up for them.

Building an architectural framework for support and feedback means setting intentional systems in place to measure how we're doing and ensure we're aligned with our family's evolving needs. It's not about perfection; it's about progress and adaptability. And like any good architect, we start by sketching out the design—by imagining the kind of father we want to be and creating structures to support that vision.

This framework of feedback and support ensures we're not navigating fatherhood alone. It equips us with the tools to reflect honestly on our actions, recalibrate based on the needs of those who matter most, and refine our approach to strengthen our bonds and help our families thrive. In the professional setting, regular check-ins and feedback cycles are non-negotiable. They're how leaders measure progress, make adjustments, and ensure their teams are working toward shared goals. Without them, even the most well-intentioned plans can veer off course, leaving people frustrated, disconnected, or worse—completely lost. Fatherhood is no different.

Just as a business leader relies on metrics to stay

aligned with their vision, a father must remain attuned to the evolving needs of his family. Life changes constantly, and so do the dynamics within your home. What worked yesterday might fall short tomorrow. What felt like enough last month might no longer be meeting the emotional, physical, or intellectual needs of your children—or your partner.

The truth is, being a father isn't just about showing up. It's about adapting. It's about asking yourself tough questions, being honest about where you're thriving and where you're falling short, and making adjustments that benefit the people who depend on you most.

Fatherhood doesn't come with a quarterly review or a performance evaluation. But maybe it should.

Why Fathers Needs a Feedback Cycle

When I think back to the weeks leading up to the birth of my daughters, I remember feeling a deep sense of uncertainty. Every week was a new challenge. Every day brought new information, new possibilities, and new fears. The only way we could navigate it all was through consistent reflection. Dr. Stewart didn't simply hope for the best—he relied on weekly check-ins, detailed observations, and a willingness to adjust his recommendations based on what he learned.

That's when it hit me.

Parenthood is one of the most important "roles" you'll ever take on. Why wouldn't it deserve the same level of intentionality we give to our professional lives? Feedback cycles allow us to pause, reflect, and recalibrate. They create space for honest self-assessment, helping us see where we're excelling, where we might need to improve, and how we can adjust to meet the ever-changing needs of our children.

Here's the truth: You don't have to be perfect to be a great father, but you do have to be present. Present enough to ask yourself questions like:
- Am I supporting my children emotionally?
- Am I creating space for them to feel safe, heard, and valued?
- Does my partner feel supported in co-parenting, or are there areas I can step up?

These questions aren't meant to shame or overwhelm you. They're intended to help you grow.

Commit to regular fatherhood check-ins—not because you're falling short, but because you care enough to want to do better. Just as a business leader measures progress and makes informed decisions, a father must reflect on his actions to ensure he's staying on the path to becoming the man and the parent he strives to be.

Fatherhood is not one-size-fits-all. It doesn't come with a manual, a blueprint, or a set of universal rules. Instead, every father shows up in his own way, shaped by his upbringing, his personality, [circum]stances, and his choices.

For some, fatherho[od] [mean]s being a provider—ensuring there's [food on] the table and a[re ove]r the family's head. For oth[ers] [it's abo]ut being pres[ent, atte]nding every soccer game, eve[ry rec]ital, every bedti[me stor]y. For others, it might still mean simply trying to survive the day without losing their patience.

Child

Partner

Personal

Feedback Loop

Depending on their age, engage your children in simple, open conversations. Ask about their favorite moments with you and what they feel could improve.

Ask your partner how they perceive your role as a father. What strengths do they see in you? Where do they think you could invest more effort?

Consider your own fatherhood KPIs. What are the key indicators that reflect how well you're doing? Maybe it's the number of meaningful conversations you have each week, or how often

The truth is there are many types of fathers. Some we admire, some we emulate, and some we struggle to understand. The goal here isn't to label or rank these types but to recognize them—to reflect on how we show up in our children's lives and to ask ourselves a simple question: Am I the father I want to be?

Because fatherhood is dynamic, it's evolving. Who you were as a father yesterday doesn't have to define who you are today, and who you are today doesn't have to limit who you can become tomorrow.

As we explore the types of fathers that exist, think about where you see yourself. Think about where you see your own father or other father figures in your life. This isn't about judgment—it's about awareness.
After all, the first step to growth is understanding where you stand.

The Traditional Father

The traditional father is often seen as the provider and disciplinarian, typically following more conventional gender roles. He may be less emotionally expressive but focuses on ensuring the family's financial stability.

Related KPI: Provision & Security

KPI Example: Measuring how well they provide for their family's needs (financial, safety, structure).

The Nurturing Father

This father is highly involved in the emotional and day-to-day care of his children. He actively nurtures, communicates, and emotionally connects with his children.

Related KPI: Emotional Intelligence & Attachment

KPI Example: Tracking the frequency and depth of meaningful conversations, shared activities, and moments of emotional support.

The Disengaged Father

A disengaged father is emotionally or physically distant. His involvement may be minimal due to work, personal challenges, or a lack of understanding of how to engage with his children.

Related KPI: Presence & Participation

KPI Example: Measuring how often and how meaningfully he engages with his children (in terms of both quantity and quality.

The Playful Father

This father focuses on fun and play, often engaging with children through games, sports, and creative activities. While this strengthens bonds, it may sometimes lack the balance of emotional or disciplinary guidance.

Related KPI: Intentional Play & Learning

KPI Example: Measuring time spent in intentional play, teaching moments, and bonding activities that encourage learning and growth.

The Disciplinarian Father

Focused on setting rules and maintaining discipline, this father often emphasizes order and respect. He tends to enforce structure and boundaries but may struggle with expressing affection or emotional availability.

Related KPI: Structure & Boundaries

KPI Example: Evaluating how well he balances discipline with warmth, ensuring clear but also fair and supportive boundaries.

The Absent Father

This father may be physically or emotionally absent from his children's lives due to separation, work, or personal circumstances. His role in his children's development may be minimal, leading to long-term challenges in their relationship.

Related KPI: Physical & Emotional Presence

KPI Example: Measuring physical availability (time spent together) and emotional presence (communication, support, understanding).

The Overinvolved Father

Description: This father tends to micromanage and heavily influence his children's decisions. While his intentions may come from love and concern, he may unintentionally stifle independence and growth.

Related KPI: Autonomy & Trust

KPI Example: Measuring how well he balances involvement with allowing his children to make decisions and learn from mistakes.

The Peer-Like Father

Description: This father strives to be his children's friend rather than a traditional parental figure. While fostering closeness, this approach may sometimes compromise authority or structure.

Related KPI: Friendship & Boundaries

KPI Example: Assessing how well he balances camaraderie with enforcing necessary boundaries and discipline.

The Workaholic Father
Description: This father prioritizes work and career over family time, often leading to limited emotional or physical availability. His contributions may lean heavily on financial provision.

Related KPI: Work-Life Balance

KPI Example: Measuring time spent with the family versus time devoted to work commitments.

The Mentor Father
Description: This father focuses on being a guide and teach-

er, emphasizing skills, values, and life lessons. He often prioritizes preparing his children for the future.

Related KPI: Life Skills & Preparation

KPI Example: Measuring the frequency of skill-building activities or lessons that prepare children for adulthood (e.g., financial literacy, problem-solving)

As you reflect on these types of fathers, you might find pieces of yourself in more than one category. That's okay—fatherhood isn't static. Some days, you might feel like the Nurturer, patiently guiding your children through life's challenges. On other days, you might slip into the role of the Ghost, struggling to be as present as you'd like to be.

What matters most is this: the willingness to reflect.

Fatherhood is a mirror, one that shows us both our strengths and our shortcomings. It's not always an easy reflection to look at, but it's one that can guide us toward becoming the men our children need.

I'll admit I've seen myself in all of these types at different points in my life. When my wife and I learned we were expecting triplets, I thought I'd be the Protector—the strong, steady presence who kept my family safe no matter the odds. But there were moments when I felt more like the Overwhelmed Father, barely holding it together.

And that's the thing about fatherhood: it's a journey, not a destination.

Fatherhood isn't just about the moments we share with our children today—it's about the legacy we leave behind. The way we show up for our kids now shapes their confidence, their resilience, and the kind of people they'll grow up to be. When I reflect on the father I want to be, it's not just about the example I'm setting—it's about the memories I'm creating. The words I want them to remember. The way I want them to feel when they think about me.

This is why we commit to the process of self-reflection and feedback—not because we're chasing perfection, but because we know the impact of our actions will ripple through generations.

So, as we move forward together, I invite you to join me in asking the hard questions, facing the truths that might not be easy, and taking the steps—big or small—to grow. Because at the end of the day, being a great father isn't about getting it right every time. It's about showing up, learning, and trying again. Every single day.

As you reflect on the types of fathers described here, think of these categories as tools for feedback—not labels to be worn permanently, but mirrors to help you see where you are and where you might want to grow. A feedback cycle isn't about getting stuck in one type; it's about noticing patterns, understanding your strengths, and finding opportunities to adapt.

Pause & Reflect

As you reflect on the types of fathers described here, think of these categories as tools for feedback—not labels to be worn permanently, but mirrors to help you see where you are and where you might want to grow. A feedback cycle isn't about getting stuck in one type; it's about noticing patterns, understanding your strengths, and finding opportunities to adapt.

1. "What type of father do I see myself as today? Circle up to three that resonate most:

Traditional	Nurturing	Disengaged
Playful	Absent	Disciplinarian
Mentor	Peer-Like	Workaholic
Overinvolved		

Why do I identify as a_____father? Take a moment to reflect on the choices, behaviors, and patterns that
have shaped your answer.

What type of father do I aspire to be?
Name the qualities or traits you want to cultivate in your
role as a father and explain why they matter to you.

How do I think my children would describe me as a father today? Reflect on what they might say about your presence, personality, and impact on their lives.

The Price of Miracles

Dr. Stewart's office was just across the street from our house, tucked within the labyrinth of a sprawling children's hospital. A place designed to inspire hope with its cheerful murals and child-sized chairs, it still managed to fill me with a quiet dread each time we walked in. By now, the once-daunting hospital complex felt almost familiar. Even the farting sound of the ultrasound gel tube, which had once made me chuckle, barely registered anymore.

The appointment began like the others—light conversation with the tech, the steady hum of the ultrasound machine, and the rhythmic thump of heartbeats filling the room. For a moment, I allowed myself to sink into the sound, letting it drown out the noise of worry swirling in my mind. But when the tech wiped off the last bit of gel and turned the lights back on, the shift was palpable. The air felt heavier, charged with unspoken tension. She exited gracefully, leaving us in silence that stretched uncomfortably thin. It felt as though we were suspended over a canyon, balancing precariously on a thread that could snap at any moment.

Dr. Stewart entered, his face composed but serious. "Let's start with Baby A," he began, pulling up the grainy ultrasound images on the screen. His tone was clinical, yet there was an edge of gravity that made my stomach tighten. "The large mass at the base of her skull," he continued, gesturing to the screen, "has not shrunk. In fact, it's larger than it was during your last visit. And her intestines still haven't retreated into her abdomen as they should have by now." The room seemed to close in on itself, but he wasn't finished. He looked at both of us, carefully weighing his following words. "If Baby A doesn't make it," he said slowly, "her physical body could still continue to grow inside the womb. In that case, you'd likely deliver her stillborn. Depending on the circumstances, surgical intervention might be necessary."

I felt Annie's grip tighten on my arm, her knuckles turning white as she absorbed the weight of his words. My mind raced, grappling with the image he'd just painted.

Dr. Stewart adjusted the screen, switching to the scans of Babies B and C. "But it's not just Baby A we're concerned about," he said, his tone steady but weighted. "Babies B and C still face significant risks. The monochorionic monoamniotic nature of this pregnancy is, by definition, high-risk. It requires a level of vigilance that goes beyond routine care."

He looked at us, carefully balancing his words. "Because the twins are sharing the same amniotic sac, the risk of cord entanglement and compression is extremely high. Without a dividing membrane, there's nothing to keep their cords from tangling, cutting off oxygen or blood flow. It's not just a possibility—it's a probability. And when complications arise in this kind of pregnancy, they can escalate very quickly."

It was as if he were a heavyweight boxing champion, and I were his sparring partner. Everything he said felt like body blows. I glanced at Annie, whose expression had hardened into a mask of quiet determination.

Dr. Stewart continued, "This is why we'll need to increase the frequency of monitoring. Initially, this will mean weekly appointments. As we approach 24 weeks, we'll likely ask you to visit the hospital for routine observation, potentially staying until delivery. The goal is to keep a close eye on all three babies, so if there's even the slightest sign of an issue, we can intervene immediately and give them the best chance of survival."

I didn't need to look or feel how what reaction Annie had to that statement. Imprisoned in a hospital for 3 months? The idea of being tethered to a hospital for months was daunting, but the alternative—missing the chance to save our children—was unthinkable. I squeezed Annie's hand, hoping the pressure would translate the words I couldn't quite form: We'll do whatever it takes.

Dr. Stewart's voice softened slightly. "This is not an easy path. I won't sugarcoat it. But the closer we get to full-term, the better the outcomes for all three babies. We're fighting for that goal—to get you as close to delivery as possible while keeping everyone safe." "There are percentages I can share with you," Dr. Stewart began, his tone careful, measured. "But I want to preface this by saying that these numbers are not certainties. They are probabilities based on what we know so far."

I felt my throat tighten, the pulse in my neck pounding like a drumbeat. Percentages. Numbers. Probabilities. These were things I could understand—things I could use to wrap my head around the chaos. And yet, as he spoke, I realized they were also things I feared. Dr. Stewart leaned forward, resting his hands on the table.

His face was lined with the gravity of what he was about to say. The room was sterile and quiet except for the hum of equipment, which seemed anxious for the words preparing to exit Dr. Stewarts mouth. Annie and I sat frozen, waiting for the words that would define the days, weeks, and months ahead. "There are numbers I need to share

with you," Dr. Stewart began, his tone cautious but steady. "I want to be clear—these are probabilities, not guarantees. But they will help us understand what we're facing."
I tightened my grip on Annie's hand, my heart pounding so hard it seemed to echo in the silence. Numbers. I could deal with numbers. Numbers had rules and boundaries. But the way he hesitated made my stomach drop.

"Baby A," he said, gesturing toward the screen. Her tiny form filled the monitor, the faint flicker of her heart-beat mesmerizing yet haunting. "She has a 70% likelihood of death at this stage. The mass at the base of her skull remains a severe concern, and her development is lagging behind."

Seventy percent. I felt hollow inside,, as if my soul were placed on a scale only to be balanced against a feather. I had a 30% chance of survival, a miracle reduced to a fraction.

I glanced at Annie, but she didn't look at me. Her gaze was locked on the screen, and her face was pale and unreadable. "And as for Babies B and C," Dr. Stewart continued, his voice softening but no less heavy with meaning, "their likelihood of death is slightly lower but still significant. They each have a 50% chance of not making it to term."

A coin toss. That's all it was—a cruel flip of the universe's coin. I felt my chest tighten, the air in the room growing heavier by the second.

Dr. Stewart hesitated, then leaned back slightly, his hands clasped in front of him. "There is another option," he said, choosing his words carefully. "If your goal is to maximize the chances of at least one baby surviving, we could consider selective reduction. It's not an easy decision, and it's not one I suggest lightly. But in high- risk pregnancies like this, it can sometimes increase the odds for the remaining babies." Selective reduction. The phrase hung in the air, cold and clinical, and yet its weight was suffocating. My mind reeled, trying to grasp the enormity of what he was saying. To choose one life over another. To decide who got a chance to live. How could anyone possibly make that choice?

Annie's grip on my hand tightened, her knuckles white. I looked at her, searching for some kind of anchor, but she was staring at the monitor, her breathing shallow. I opened my mouth to say something, anything, but no words came. All I could hear was the faint, rhythmic thrum of three fragile heartbeats—a sound both miraculous and devastating.

Dr. Stewart's voice broke through the silence, calm but firm. "This isn't a decision you have to make today," he said. "Take time. Think it over. Talk to each other. And know that whatever you choose, we'll do everything in our power to support you and your babies."

The room fell silent once again, the gravity of his words pressing down on us like a suffocating weight. In that moment, I realized this wasn't just a medical challenge—it was an emotional and moral battlefield, one we were being forced to navigate without a map. The stakes weren't just high; they were everything.

"Doctor," I said, my voice feeling horse from all my silent screaming, "are the kids in pain?"
This time, his expression faltered. It was subtle—a flicker in his eyes, a tightening of his jaw—but it was there. The kind of crack that reveals the humanity beneath the armor. He took a moment before answering, his voice softer now, more measured. "No," he said, meeting my gaze. "At this stage, they don't feel pain the way we do. But that doesn't make this any easier." The word felt hollow, like a cruel joke. Nothing about this was easy. Not the uncertainty, not the fear, not the helplessness of knowing that so much of what was to come was beyond our control.

He continued, his voice soft but firm. "According to state law, you can opt to selectively reduce up until week 20. However, I didn't feel comfortable performing the procedure in the past week 17." He glanced at the clock on the wall. "That gives you approximately two and a half weeks to make a decision.

Two and a half weeks.
Seventeen days.
Four hundred and eight hours.

I felt the countdown begin immediately, like a timer had been set in the background of my mind.

I thanked him for his candor and honesty, for being our guide through a labyrinth filled with unexpected traps and lurking minotaurs. His job wasn't easy, and I knew he wasn't taking any of this lightly.

I don't remember standing up or walking out of the room and down the hallway. All I remember is the weight. The crushing, suffocating weight of being a parent—not the joys or celebrations we often associate with the title, but the impossible, soul-crushing decisions that come with it. It's a weight no one prepares you for. No parenting book covers this. No advice column offers guidance for when your children's lives are measured in percentages, timelines, and probabilities. As Annie and I walked out into the parking lot, the sunlight seemed harsher than before. The warmth didn't comfort me; it felt like it was burning straight through me. For the first time, I truly understood that being a parent isn't just about love. It's about bearing the weight of choices that feel too big for you, too heavy for anyone.
Two and a half weeks. That was all we had.

On the drive home from the hospital, Annie and I discussed how best to inform our parents. We decided on a calm, calculated, factual approach—one rooted in the evidence Dr. Stewart had provided, stripped of the raw emotions we were barely beginning to process ourselves.
It wasn't because we didn't trust them. It wasn't because we didn't need their support. But both of our parents are deeply religious. My father-in-law is a prominent preacher within our denomination, a man whose sermons move entire con-

gregations, and my parents have been stalwarts of the faith for decades. We knew that sharing this news wouldn't just open us up to the solace of prayer—it would invite questions. Lots of questions. Questions about faith. Questions about prayer. Questions about our faith and prayer.

For the first time in my life, religion felt intrusive. It didn't feel like the private, intimate refuge it had always been. Instead, it felt like a spotlight shining on our pain, exposing it to a larger community that would inevitably want answers—answers we didn't have.

I didn't want to talk to my religious friends. I didn't want to entertain questions about what I was praying for, how often I was praying, or what my plan was. The truth was, I couldn't process anything more than what I'd already heard in that doctor's office.

When I'm stressed—truly stressed—I retreat inward. It's a safety mechanism, a survival instinct, like a body conserving blood in the core to prevent hypothermia. I cut off anything and anyone that might interfere with my process, including the well-meaning questions of people who love me.

What I hadn't fully considered, though, was the ripple effect. This wasn't just a stone thrown into the calm waters of our lives—it was a boulder. And the ripples would soon become waves.

The Day that Silence Fell

It was April 22, 1981, a mild spring day in Owosso, Oklahoma. The temperature hovered around a comfortable 64 degrees, the kind of weather that makes you want to leave your windows open and savor the breeze. Vladimir, just two years and eight months old, was a bright spark of energy. He had a voice that often carried through the house, singing songs he'd pieced together from the world around him. More than just a lively toddler, Vladimir was a helper, eager to carry small bags or offer his little hands to tidy up.

That day, my mother and Vladimir returned from a routine grocery run. The driveway of our house sloped gently downward, a feature so unremarkable it barely registered in day-to-day life. They were driving an Oldsmobile Cutlass, a sturdy car by appearance but known for its quirks—its transmission, in particular, had a reputation for being less than reliable. At the time, it was just another detail in the rhythm of their afternoon, a passing thought in a day that seemed like any other.

As my mother carried the groceries inside, Vladimir lingered near the car, his boundless curiosity guiding him as it always did. Maybe he had spotted something shiny on the floor or remembered a toy tucked under the seat. At just shy of three years old, he loved to play, his imagination as vivid as the Oklahoma sky above him.

He probably climbed into the front seat, gripping the wheel like a race car driver, making engine noises with his lips. To him, the Oldsmobile Cutlass wasn't just a car—it was a rocket ship, a getaway vehicle, a chariot for adventure. The dashboard lights and levers must have looked like a pilot's controls, tempting him to explore further.

As Vladimir sat behind the wheel, his tiny hands gripping it with the conviction of a seasoned driver, he was no longer in our driveway—he was racing in the Grand Prix

500. The Oldsmobile Cutlass, in all its rusty brown glory, was his rocket ship, a vehicle of imagination as vivid as his dreams. He leaned forward, twisting the wheel and mimicking the roar of an engine, a wide grin spread across his face. But then, something shifted. The car, once stationary, began to inch forward, the faint slope of the driveway suddenly coming alive. Startled, Vladimir froze for a moment, the reality of the situation breaking through his fantasy. He must have realized the movement wasn't part of his game. Not wanting to get in trouble, he scrambled to get out of the car.

The insignificant slope in the driveway was anything but—this old brown rocket ship was about to take off. His small hands fumbled for balance as he tried to escape the moving vehicle. In the chaos, his footing gave way, and the car's weight, indifferent and unyielding, moved forward. The moment became a blur of innocence colliding with inevitability.

Inside, my mother was putting away groceries, likely expecting to hear his cheerful voice at any moment, a request for a snack or a new song. But instead, there was nothing—no familiar noise of a happy child, the kind of silence that feels unnatural, even wrong, when there's a child in the house.

She called his name once and twice, but there was no response. The silence stretched, becoming heavier with each passing second. My mother stepped outside, her heart beginning to pound.

And then she saw him.

Vladimir lay beneath the car's tire, motionless. My mother's scream was a sound no one on that quiet street would ever forget. It wasn't just a cry of shock or fear—it was something primal, a sound pulled from the deepest corners of grief. Neighbors came running, drawn by her wails. One called the ambulance, their voice steady despite the panic swelling in the air.

Emergency vehicles soon filled the street. Flashing lights painted the scene red and blue, a chaotic contrast to the devastating stillness on the ground. As first responders worked, my father, who had lent my mother their only car, was already at work, having gotten a ride from a nearby neighbor.

The neighbor's wife made the first call. Her words were calm but carried an urgency that sent a chill down her husband's spine. "Get him home now," she said. When my father asked what had happened, the neighbor chose his words carefully. "There's been an incident," he replied, avoiding specifics. "You need to go home. Now."

The drive back must have felt endless. Each second stretched unbearably, as though time itself was conspiring to keep him from the answers he desperately needed. Every turn felt slower than the last, and every passing mile was a cruel reminder of how far he still was from his family.

When my father finally arrived, he was greeted by chaos. Flashing lights bathed the driveway in relentless red and blue, their rhythm pulsing like an urgent heartbeat. First responders moved quickly, their voices a flurry of controlled urgency. Amid it all was my mother, crumpled on the curb, her body trembling with grief. She couldn't lift her head to meet my father's gaze. Her sobs came in waves, raw and unfiltered, each one threatening to drown the air between them.

And then he saw it.

There, etched into the driveway like a scar, was a small chalk outline. It was unmistakable, its presence cutting through the confusion with brutal clarity. As the ambulance doors slammed shut and the sirens began to wail, my father watched it disappear down the street. The sound faded, but the weight of what it carried lingered.

He didn't stop to ask questions. Instead, he climbed into the passenger seat of a waiting police car, his focus singular. "Take me to the hospital," he said, his voice steady despite the storm brewing inside him.

The hospital was a blur of sterile hallways and muted whispers. My father moved through it with a single-minded determination, stopping nurses and doctors, his voice unwavering yet desperate. "Where is my son?" he repeated, the question hanging in the air like an unanswered prayer.

Finally, they led him to the pediatric wing. He

stepped through the door, calling Vladimir's name softly as if his voice alone could summon life back into the room. When his hand reached out to touch his son, he was met with the cold stillness of reality. The truth settled over him like a shroud, final and inescapable.

Vladimir was gone.

The Ripple Effect

When I told my father about the complications with our pregnancy—the 30% chance that Baby A might survive, the coin toss odds for Babies B and C, and the near certainty that we could lose all three—his reaction wasn't solely about the triplets. It was about Vladimir.

I saw it in his face the moment I finished speaking. His eyes softened, filled with a sorrow that ran deeper than words could express. His jaw tightened as if holding back the weight of memories that threatened to overwhelm him. My father wasn't just hearing news of a difficult pregnancy. He was reliving a pain he had buried long ago, a grief so profound it had shaped the man he had become.

In his mind, there was no question of whether or not he would rally. The same man who had spent decades preparing us for the inevitability of his own passing—carefully planning, protecting, and providing for his family—now mobilized every resource, every ounce of strength, to shield us from a pain he knew too well. This wasn't just about the triplets. It was about his resolve to ensure no father in his family would bear the same weight he had carried all these years.

But for me, his swift, almost mechanical response felt overwhelming. I wasn't ready for action plans or logistical solutions. I wasn't ready for anything, really.
I wasn't prepared for the ripple effect this news would create—for how the tragedy of my father's past would collide with the uncertainty of my present.

As I sat there, caught between my father's resolve and my own paralysis, I couldn't help but feel the weight of silence once again.

The silence of the car rolling.
The silence of unanswered questions.
The silence between what was and what could be.

It was a silence that spoke louder than anything else.

My mom was pregnant with my older brother, Mathieu, at the time of Vladimir's death. The grief that followed the loss of their firstborn cast a shadow so vast it seemed to eclipse the very air she breathed. She couldn't eat. She wouldn't eat. The sorrow was so overwhelming that it consumed her entirely, draining her will to move forward. There were serious conversations about how to force-feed her if she didn't begin eating soon.
The doctors were clear: she had to survive be-

cause there was another baby who needed her. Mathieu was depending on her strength, even if she had none left for herself. That reality became the tether that pulled her back, one fragile strand at a time, keeping her grounded in a world that now felt unbearable. She carried the weight of grief while also carrying the fragile hope of new life, an impossible balancing act that only a mother could endure.

Years later, we lived in the echoes of that grief. As children, we didn't fully understand it, but it was a presence that lingered in our home, quiet but undeniable. I remember being around ten years old, watching my mom hold Mathieu's hands. She would rub them gently, almost reverently, her eyes clouded with something I couldn't name. Then, the tears would come. "He has such beautiful hands," she'd whisper through her sobs. "Such magical hands."

At the time, it baffled me. What could be so special about hands? Why did this simple gesture unravel her so completely? But as I grew older, I understood. Those moments weren't just about Mathieu's hands—they were about Vladimir's. They were about the tiny hands she would never hold again, the fingers that never got the chance to grow into the same magical beauty she now saw in Mathieu's. Grief doesn't explain itself—it lives in the quiet moments, in gestures, in things left unsaid. My mother's sorrow shaped the rhythm of our lives, an unspoken companion that left its fingerprints on everything we touched.

My father, on the other hand, would walk up the

sloped driveway where the tragedy had occurred. He stopped at the spot where his son had died, standing motionless, lost in a storm of anger, sadness, and despair.

Out of the corner of his eye, he noticed a car pull up to the curb. A large man stepped out and began walking toward him. My dad didn't move. He didn't speak. He didn't know what to expect.

Without a word, the stranger opened his arms and embraced my father. It wasn't a polite, distant hug—it was the kind of embrace that swallows you whole, absorbs your broken pieces, and holds them together. My father never said how long they stood there, but I imagine time stood still. They embraced until my father's ocean of grief poured out through his tears. They embraced until my father, who moments earlier had felt entirely alone in the world, found a sliver of hope.

When it was over, the man said nothing. He simply returned to his car and drove away.
To this day, my father refers to him as an angel. He says that solitary moment saved his life.
But it also left him with a regret he would carry for 38 years.

The Albatross of Regret

The day the stranger came was the day my father became a devout Christian. Hope pulled him from the razor's edge of pain to a man with feelings and purpose. The guilt that had him in a stranglehold wasn't just that he wasn't there for his family in a time of crisis; it was that if he had more faith, God would have saved his son. If his faith had been stronger, if his prayers had been more earnest, if his conviction had been unwavering, Vladimir would have opened his eyes, stood up from the gurney, and walked into his arms.

But he didn't pray for a miracle. He didn't even ask. That regret has been the albatross around his neck ever since—a weight he carries in moments of stillness, a shadow that haunts his thoughts.

So when this crisis arose with his third son—my family—he saw it not just as a moment to act but as an opportunity to right the wrong he believed he had committed decades before. His course of action was immediate, uncompromising, and entirely his own.

My father decided to fast for one week without being asked or told. No food. No water. Just prayer. He saw this as his chance to prove his faith, to show the conviction he believed he had lacked before. At this point in his life, my father was battling his own health concerns. But none of that mattered to him.

For my father, this wasn't just about prayer—it was about redemption.

My mom, understandably concerned, begged him to

stop. She pleaded with him to drink water or rest during the hottest parts of the day. But my father is stubborn and persistent—qualities deeply embedded in our genetic material. He had spent the past decade preparing his body for a healthy, longer life. After becoming vegan, he had grown his own produce in the backyard, tending to his garden with care and pride. But now, under the punishing Texas spring heat, he was pushing his body to its absolute limits.

By the third day of his fast, my father began sending me daily emails, pages upon pages of updates—his prayers, reflections and hopes for the triplets.

I couldn't read them. Not because I didn't care but because I couldn't handle it. I told my mom to make him to stop. Whatever decision Annie and I made—whether we chose to selectively reduce or continue the pregnancy—it was our decision alone. And yet, I knew his emails weren't about influencing our choice. They were his way of processing his grief, of channeling his energy into something tangible.

While my father fasted, prayed, and poured his entire being into those emails, I found myself paralyzed by the weight of the decision in front of us.

How do you choose who should live and who shouldn't? How do you decide to intervene or not intervene in something as fragile as a 30% chance of survival?

The truth was, I couldn't choose. I wasn't capable of it. So I didn't.

I told myself we would make no decision until we had an update from Dr. Stewart. Until then, we waited—clinging to hope, fighting off fear, and pretending that time wasn't running out. In the end, the choice was never fully mine to make. It felt like the universe, fate, or whatever higher power you believe in would move the pieces for us. As we waited for our next appointment with Dr. Stewart, I couldn't shake the feeling that our lives and choices were now part of a narrative that had begun decades earlier. My father, driven by a desire to rewrite the past, took on a burden he didn't need to bear. I understood his motivations, but I couldn't allow his mission to dictate my own.

As we sat waiting for our next appointment with Dr. Stewart, I couldn't shake the feeling that our lives and choices were now part of a narrative that had begun decades earlier.

Decision Day

We got dressed, one foot at a time, just like any other day. We ate—barely—with utensils that felt foreign in our hands. We drove to the hospital, navigating the familiar streets in stillness, neither of us brave enough to voice the swirling thoughts in our heads.

We greeted the nurse, the same one with triplets of her own, and exchanged half-hearted pleasantries. She smiled at us the way someone does when they know they're a lifeline in a storm, but the weight in the room was heavy enough to silence even her usual cheer. Back in the exam room, the routine played out as always. The sound of the ultrasound gel forced out of the tube with that faint, familiar farting noise. The lights dimmed as the ultrasound machine flickered to life. The quiet rustle of paper as Annie adjusted herself on the exam table.

But there was no laughter this time. No jokes about striations or pretending to read the shadows on the screen. The humor we once clung to had dissolved under the gravity of what was at stake.

We waited.

The seconds dragged, the silence punctuated only by the faint hum of the machine. And then Dr. Stewart entered. He was prompt as always, his movements steady, his presence grounded. Yet even his entrance, which usually brought a sense of calm, felt different today. There was no air in the room. It wasn't that we weren't breathing—we had to be to stay alive—but it felt as though every molecule of oxygen had been vacuumed out, leaving nothing but a suffocating stillness.

The Moment of Truth

Dr. Stewart moved to the ultrasound machine without a preamble. We didn't make small talk. We didn't try to lighten the mood. We waited, watching the screen as his steady hand guided the wand across Annie's belly.

When the image of Baby A appeared, he paused.
For a moment, the only sound was the faint thump-thump-thump of a heartbeat on the monitor. My palms were sweating, and my legs were pulsating, but I couldn't tell if it was from fear or hope—or both. Dr. Stewart turned to us, his eyes searching ours, and said, "I cannot explain to you what I'm looking at. What I can tell you is this: the intestines have successfully receded inside the body, and there is no longer a hygroma at the base of the skull. This is a miracle." He paused, giving us time to process. "Baby A," he continued, "is out of the window of danger."

Still, no gasp. No exhale of air. Annie and I remained frozen as if we were too afraid to fully believe what we had just heard. Dr. Stewart didn't linger on the moment. He moved the wand again, shifting the screen to check on Babies B and C. "The condition remains stable for now," he said, his voice calm and steady. "There's nothing to be concerned with at this time."

Finally, he turned to us with a small smile and said, "I want to congratulate you. You have three healthy babies."

May 31st, 2016 Week 17.

Two words: healthy babies.

It took a moment for the words to settle in, for my

auditory process to triple-check what we heard, and for me to feel a signal of relief throughout my body. I glanced at Annie, whose eyes were still locked on the screen, her expression frozen between shock and relief. I squeezed her hand, trying to ground myself, but I still couldn't breathe—not fully.

38 years 1 month 9 day

One life taken, one life riddled with grief, but three lives spared. The significance of the moment rippled through me like an electric current. My father's grief, his endless prayers, his decade- spanning albatross—all of it felt vindicated in that instant.

38 years earlier, my family's world was shattered. For decades, he carried that grief like a ghost strapped to his back. He mourned in silence, lived in the shadow of what could have been, and bore the crushing regret of never asking for a miracle.

But on this day, his ghosts were buried.

It was as if he had seen the future because two days earlier, he had already told us—with conviction—that everything would be fine. I didn't want to believe him at the time. His faith, unwavering and absolute, had felt almost naïve in the face of such overwhelming odds. But now, sitting in that room, staring at the images of our three babies, I realized he had been right.

Relief.

Dr. Stewart handed us the ultrasound images and gave us a few final words of reassurance before leaving the room. I don't remember much of what he said. All I could hear was the echo of those three words: healthy baby girls. Annie and I sat there momentarily, the silence now warm instead of suffocating. She looked at me, her eyes brimming with tears, and for the first time in weeks, I saw her shoulders relax.

The weight of decision day lifted, replaced by something else entirely—something lighter, freer, and filled with possibility.

We didn't say much to each other on the way home. There was no need. For the first time in what felt like forever, there was no crisis to solve, no numbers to calculate, no choices to agonize over.
There was only gratitude.

Building Your Fatherhood Support System

Parenthood, especially fatherhood, is a journey that can sometimes feel isolating. The challenges you face—balancing work, relationships, and the needs of your children—are uniquely yours, but they're also universally shared by other dads. That's where the power of a support system comes into play.

Building a feedback loop with your family is essential for growth, but no father can thrive in isolation. Just as we ask our children or partners for input, we must also look outward—to our communities, friends, and mentors—for the guidance, encouragement, and wisdom we need to succeed. But not all support is created equal. Choosing the right people to lean on can make the difference between stagnation and transformation.

Choosing the Right People to Support You

When it comes to building a support system, intentionality is everything. Think of your network as a garden—what you nurture will grow. Surrounding yourself with the right people can help you maintain focus, push through challenges, and show up for your family in meaningful ways. Here's how to choose wisely:

Seek Out Trusted Advisors

Look for individuals who have walked the path before you. They don't have to be perfect fathers, but they should embody qualities you admire—whether it's patience, resilience, or the ability to balance work and family life. Mentors can offer perspective, share hard-earned lessons, and remind you that you're not alone in the struggles or joys of fatherhood.

Cultivate Reciprocal Relationships

Support isn't just about what others can do for you—it's about creating a mutual exchange. Surround yourself with people who not only lift you up but also allow you to give back. The act of supporting others—whether it's a fellow dad, a struggling friend, or your partner— strengthens your own sense of purpose and community.

Prioritize Growth-Oriented Connections

Growth happens when you're challenged. Choose relationships that encourage you to stretch outside your comfort zone. This might mean joining a parenting group, reconnecting with friends who inspire you, or becoming part of a community like Elevate Fatherhood, where like-minded dads come together to learn, grow, and celebrate wins both big and small.

Avoid Negative Influences

Not all advice is good, and not all relationships are positive. Be mindful of people who dismiss your efforts, reinforce harmful stereotypes about fatherhood, or discourage you from striving for more. Your support system should empower you, not hold you back.

The Elevate Fatherhood Community

One of the most powerful ways to cultivate support is by joining a community of fathers committed to personal growth and family excellence. The Elevate Fatherhood community was designed with this in mind—a space where dads can share stories, exchange strategies, and inspire one another to reach their potential.

Whether you're looking for advice on managing work-life balance, tips for fostering emotional intelligence in your children, or just a place to celebrate wins, Elevate Fatherhood is here to help. Through regular discussions, resources, and events, the Elevate Fatherhood community focuses on two key pillars:

1. Personal Development: Providing tools and strategies to help you grow as an individual and as a father.
2. Community Engagement: Connecting you with other dads who understand the journey and can offer perspective, encouragement, and camaraderie.

As fathers, we owe it to ourselves—and to our children—to build the strongest foundation possible. That foundation starts with feedback, reflection, and recalibration within our own families. But it extends outward to include a network of people who inspire, guide, and challenge us to be the best versions of ourselves. Choose your community wisely, and remember: You're not alone on this journey. Together, we can elevate fatherhood to new heights.

Part III

"Control your passions before your passions control you."

My Father, Lawrence May

Mastering Emotional intelligence

In the summer of 1989, my family moved from the United States to a small town just north of Paris, France. It was an adventure in every sense of the word—a chance to explore a new culture, language, and way of life. However, for a child, the comforts of home can be hard to leave behind. For me, those comforts came in the form of Jolly Ranchers, Oreos, and cookies-and-cream ice cream. Living overseas meant these American treats were rare delicacies, only arriving when visiting family members carried them across the Atlantic in their suitcases. So when a fresh package of Oreos appeared in our cupboard one day, it felt like striking gold.

Late one night, when the house was quiet and everyone else was fast asleep, I snuck down to the kitchen. I told myself I'd just take one Oreo—just one taste to satisfy the craving. But one became two. Two became a handful. Each bite was like a tiny rebellion, a sweet, stolen thrill.
The next evening, after dinner, my mom excitedly announced dessert: Oreos. My father walked over to the cupboard, oblivious to my late-night heist, and pulled out the package. To my horror, I wasn't the only one who had indulged. Someone else had also given in to temptation, leaving the package far too empty for comfort. My father's reaction was swift and unrelenting. "You let your hunger control you," he said. Our punishment?

1 Oreo cookie = 2 hours of in-room grounding.

At the time, I thought the punishment was cruel. I stewed in my room, replaying every bite in my mind, wondering how I had let my cravings get the best of me. But as I grew older, I realized the lesson wasn't about the cookies—it was about self-control. My father wasn't just punishing us for sneaking a snack; he was teaching us to master our impulses before they mastered us.

Reflecting on that moment, I realize it was a small

yet powerful illustration of my father's parenting style. He wasn't merely raising children; he was cultivating character. He recognized that self-control, discipline, and emotional regulation were essential skills we would need long after our childhood.

My father's voice echoes in my mind every time I reflect on the lessons he tried to instill in me: "Control your passions before your passions control you." It was more than advice—it was a blueprint for emotional intelligence. At its core, emotional intelligence is about recognizing your emotions, understanding their power, and learning to manage them in ways that align with your values. My father's mantra was his way of teaching us to master self-control, a skill that would serve us not just in childhood but for the rest of our lives.

I was well into my 30s when a conversation with my cousin on my father's side shed light on the deeper origins of this saying. My father, the second oldest of 12 siblings, was shaped by a family history riddled with love and dysfunction. My grandfather—affectionately described as a "rolling stone"—left behind a complicated legacy. Generations of May men had built multiple families, often in the same city or neighborhood, creating cycles of chaos that affected relationships and worldviews. In no way am I casting stones or disparaging what afflicts many families. Marriage is hard, and divorce is devastating. My father and I both failed at our first attempts at marriage. His resulted in two half-brothers I've recently connected with, as they are much older than me.

Both of my parents, perhaps in response to this dysfunction,
were determined to raise us with strict boundaries. They
put the fear of God in me when it came to sex and responsibility. Despite my strong religious convictions as a teenager,
it wasn't lost on me—and my brothers—that there would be
dire consequences if we fathered a child before we were
stable, reliable, and capable of providing.

You're about to die laughing.

In both Christian and Jewish traditions, there's a
story about Joseph, the 11th son of Jacob, who was sold
into slavery by his brothers. While serving in the household
of Potiphar, a prominent nobleman in Egypt, Joseph found
himself the target of Potiphar's wife's advances. She repeat-
edly tried to seduce him, but Joseph resisted, ultimately
fleeing her grasp—leaving his tunic in her hands as he ran.
Now imagine growing up with your mother, from age five
until adulthood, consistently telling you, "If you're ever in a
predicament like Joseph, R-U-N!" It felt more like a comical
reminder than a severe warning at the time, but that lesson
lodged itself in my subconscious
like gum on a shoe.

Fast forward to college. At 20, I juggled school and
late-night shifts at a call center where I worked while relish-
ing the newfound freedom of living independently for the

first time. One evening, a God-fearing young lady invited me over for dinner. IFYKYK

The aroma of home-cooked chicken filled the air, mingling with the comforting scent of freshly baked bread. The table was set like something out of a holiday dinner—a feast made with care and intention. It was the kind of spread that could make you forget every worry, the weight of the day melting away with every bite. I walked in with good intentions, fully resolved to keep things "vegetarian," with no insertions of any kind. But, as is often the case when desire and temptation sit down at the same table, my resolve was about to be tested.

Dinner was perfect—a symphony of flavors accompanied by easy conversation and lingering glances. We laughed between bites, her eyes catching mine in a way that made my pulse quicken. By the time the plates were cleared, I'd convinced myself that everything was under control. After all, we were just two friends catching up. Nothing more.

That conviction lasted until the couch.

It started innocently enough. We were sitting close, laughing about old stories and sharing memories. But then the jokes became more personal, the laughter softer, her hand brushing mine in a way that wasn't accidental. The tension grew like a storm gathering on the horizon—silent but undeniable. A playful nudge became a lingering touch;

suggestive flirting led to heavy petting, and before I knew it, we were kissing with an intensity that left no room for ambiguity.

In the periphery of my vision, a mirror caught the reflection of us—myself, disheveled and undeniably at full salute. There I was, caught in a battle between head and body, logic and instinct. It was the kind of moment where time seemed to slow, where every second stretched into eternity. Somewhere in the recesses of my mind, a voice whispered, just once, maybe twice... But that voice was quickly drowned out by the rush of adrenaline and the fire spreading through every nerve.

Clothes fell away like leaves in the wind. The next thing I knew, I was as bare as Adam and Eve on the day they were created. And just like that, the line I swore I wouldn't cross had disappeared behind me. And then, like a guardian angel disguised as my childhood memories, I heard my mom's voice in my head—this time as an exaggerated juvenile sing-song: "You better run for it, run for, RUN!" I snapped back to reality, grabbed my clothes and shoes, hurdled over the furniture like an Olympic sprinter, and bolted to my car. By the time I was safely inside and driving away, my heart pounded like a drum. I couldn't help but laugh at the absurdity of it all. The situation was both ridiculous and humbling, but it brought me face-to-face with a deeper understanding of the lessons my parents had worked so hard to instill in me.

At that moment, I didn't just hear my mother's words; I understood their purpose. Emotional intelligence isn't simply about restraint—it's about making decisions that align with the values you want to live by. It's about pausing to reflect, recalibrate, and refine before emotions take the wheel.

When my father told me to "control your passions," he wasn't just offering advice. He handed me a roadmap for navigating a world that would test me in ways I couldn't imagine. But like all roadmaps, it wasn't perfect. My father's lessons were shaped by his fears, traumas, and triumphs. They molded me in ways I'm grateful for, but they also left me with a choice: to continue his legacy where it served me and to break free from the parts that didn't.

Breaking Generational Cycles

As fathers, we face a two-fronted battle.
On one side, we're tasked with honoring the positive attributes of the men who poured into us—whether it's our fathers, grandfathers, or father figures who shaped us. Their wisdom, their strength, and their sacrifices deserve to be acknowledged and celebrated.

On the other side, we carry the responsibility of ending generational curses—the cycles of hurt, trauma, or dysfunction that we might unintentionally pass on to our children if we're not careful. It's not an easy task. Our characters are molded by the experiences of those who came before us, but we are not bound to replicate their mistakes. If your childhood was fraught with challenges, you are not destined to recreate those experiences for your own children. Conversely, even if you grew up in an idyllic environment, there's no guarantee you'll be able to replicate it exactly. But remember, we are not bound by our pasts. We are only bound by what we choose to cultivate. And the power to break free from negative cycles lies within us.

We have a rare and powerful opportunity to reflect on our upbringing and decide what to carry forward and leave behind. This isn't about seeking perfection but showing up with intention and commitment to grow. The process starts with reflection—a moment of honesty with yourself. Think about the lessons your father or father figure taught you. Which of these lessons shaped you for the better? Which of them might you need to unlearn?

From there, it's about recalibrating. Ask yourself, "What kind of father do I want to be?" This question isn't just a goal—it's a guiding principle that can shape your actions, decisions, and relationships. Growth happens when you take those reflections and refine your approach, one intentional step at a time.

What kind of father do I want to be?
Reflection Questions for Growth
To help you start this process, here are a few questions to

guide your journey:

The journey of fatherhood is not about perfection—it's about progress. It's about showing up, being honest with yourself, and doing the work to grow for the sake of your children.

Remember, the legacy you leave isn't just in the lessons you teach but in how you live. Let your actions, words, and willingness to grow to be the roadmap your children follow.

Pause & Reflect

Who in your life modeled emotional intelligence for you, and what did you learn from them?

How effective are you at regulating your emotions? On a scale from 1-10, where 1 denotes the least amount of control, and 10 represents mastery of control.

What are the most valuable lessons I learned from my father (or a father figure), and how do I plan to pass them on to my children?

What patterns or behaviors from my upbringing do I not want to replicate in my own parenting?

How have my experiences with injustice or adversity shaped my outlook on life and parenting?

What does emotional health mean to me, and how can I foster it within my family?

In what ways can I actively make space for my children to forge their own paths, distinct from my experiences?

How can I ensure that the successes I strive for in parenting are aligned with what is genuinely best for my children's well-being and happiness?

What steps can I take to learn from the past while building a positive and hopeful future for my family?

Navigating Emotions with Kids

Parenting is like stepping into the most immersive and unpredictable classroom you'll ever experience. There's no syllabus, no cheat sheet, just real-time lessons taught by pint-sized professors whose moods shift faster than the weather. One moment, they're beaming with pride over a finger-painting masterpiece; the next, they're inconsolable because you cut their sandwich into triangles instead of squares. The truth is, raising children isn't just about shaping their world—it's about learning to navigate the ever-changing landscape of their emotions, as well as your own.

Emotions are tricky things, much like trying to explain to an ice cream cone why it shouldn't melt in the summer sun. Paul Eckman, a pioneer in psychology, once boiled down human emotions into six core feelings:

| Surprised | Anger | Happiness |
| Sadness | Fear | Disgust |

This list might seem like it covers the bases, but emotions are anything but simple.

In 2017, Drs. Cowen and Keltner expanded on Eckman's work with groundbreaking research. They analyzed reactions to 2,185 short video clips, uncovering the vast emotional spectrum humans experience. Their study revealed 27 distinct emotional dimensions, from awe to frustration, joy to despair. These aren't just abstract concepts—they're the building blocks of your child's emotional world, the very feelings they wrestle with daily.

Admiration	Adoration	Aesthetic	Apprecia-tion
Amuse-ment	Anger	Aniexty	Awkward-ness
Calmness	Confusion	Craving	Digust
Entrance-ment	Empathic Pain	Excitement	Fear
Horror	Interest	Joy	Nostalgia
Relief	Romance	Sadness	Satisfaction
Sexual Desiire	Surprise		

Raising kids is like a rollercoaster that's equal parts exhilarating and terrifying. Kids are these incredible beings of pure emotion, untamed and unfiltered. One minute, they're bundles of joy, giggling away to glory, and the next, they're the embodiment of rage over something as simple as the wrong color of a cup.

The key? Patience, understanding, and a whole lot of emotional intelligence. Emotional intelligence isn't just about controlling your feelings—it's about understanding them. It's recognizing your emotions, figuring out where they come from, and managing them in ways that align with your values. For us as fathers, it's not just about having that awareness—it's about showing our kids how to do the same. And it's not one big, dramatic lesson. It happens in the small, everyday moments.

After reflecting on my father's lessons and the emotional legacy I want to pass on to my kids, I realized that how we show up matters just as much as why. Modeling emotional intelligence isn't just something we hope they'll absorb—it's something we need to teach and reinforce. And one of the most effective tools I've found for this is what I call emotional check-ins.

Turning Lessons into Rituals

Let's discuss emotional check-ins. They're simple but intentional moments that create space for conversations about feelings. Emotional check-ins are not rocket science, but they do require you to pause and be present.

Imagine this:

A father and his 11-year-old son are walking home from school. The dad starts with the usual questions:

"How was school?"

"Did you have enough to eat for lunch?"

"Do you have any homework?"

The son gives short, typical answers: "Fine," "Yes," "Not much." But then the father decides to try something new—he opens up about his own day.

Father: "I was running on the treadmill today and got into a friendly competition with the person next to me."

Son: "Dad, that's so random."

Father: "I struggle with mundane tasks like running. I know it's good for me, but I get bored, so I find ways to stay engaged."

Son: "I've never thought about that before."

Father: "Is there a time during school when you start to feel bored?"

Son: "During math class right after lunch. It's always so hot in the room, plus I sit at the back of the class and can barely hear the teacher."

In that moment, the father has created an opportunity—not just to understand his son's experience but to model emotional awareness.

How to Make Emotional Check-ins Work

The key to turning emotional check-ins into valuable conversations is to listen more than you talk. Here are a few steps to guide you:

1. Listen for feeling words. If your child mentions frustration, boredom, or excitement, dig into that.
2. Confirm you've understood their feelings. Say something like, "It sounds like you're frustrated because it's hard to hear the teacher in math class."
3. Ask follow-up questions. Get specific: "What do you think would help you feel more engaged in math?"
4. Build trust by thanking them for sharing. A simple "Thanks for telling me about that" goes a long way.
5. Transition to solutions together. After acknowledging their emotions, ask, "What's one thing we could do to make this better?"

Modeling Emotional Intelligence

Kids are incredible imitators. They soak up what we do far more than what we say. That's why modeling emotional intelligence is the most powerful tool we have as fathers. Show them it's okay to feel joy, sadness, fear, and triumph—and teach them how to process those feelings in a healthy way.

Here's how you can model emotional intelligence in your daily life:

1. Name Your Emotions: "I'm feeling frustrated because I had a tough day."
2. Listen Actively: Show empathy by listening without interrupting.
3. Demonstrate Healthy Coping: Use positive strategies like taking deep breaths or going for a walk when emotions run high.
4. pologize When Needed: "I'm sorry I lost my temper earlier. I'll do better next time."
5. Be Empathetic: Acknowledge others' feelings: "That must have been hard for them."
6. Discuss Emotions Through Stories: Use books or movies to talk about what characters might be feeling.
7. Set Emotional Boundaries: Calmly express when you need space: "I need a moment to think before I respond."
8. Praise Effort Over Outcome: "I'm proud of how you worked through that problem, even though it was tough."
9. Stay Calm in Conflict: Model problem-solving during

disagreements.

10. Reflect Together: After emotional moments, talk about what helped and what didn't.

Emotional Resilience

Emotional resilience is at the heart of emotional intelligence—the ability to bounce back from setbacks. Teaching our kids resilience isn't about shielding them from failure; it's about showing them how to rise after they fall.

Steps to Build Emotional Resilience Together:

1. Acknowledge Feelings: Let your kids know it's okay to feel frustrated, sad, or scared.
2. Model Problem-Solving: Approach challenges together with a calm, step-by-step attitude.
3. Celebrate Effort: Focus on persistence, not just results.
4. Normalize Mistakes: Share your own missteps and what you learned from them.
5. Use Positive Self-Talk: Teach them to encourage themselves during tough moments.
6. Adapt to Change: Show flexibility and help them see alternatives when plans shift.

Connecting Emotional Intelligence and Resilience

Emotional intelligence isn't just a skill for managing the moment—it's the foundation for building a lifetime of resilience. As fathers, every emotional check-in, every modeled moment, every conversation about feelings lays a brick in the foundation of who our children become.

When we take the time to reflect on our own emotional patterns, recalibrate how we respond, and refine our approach as parents, we not only teach emotional intelligence—we live it.

So here's my challenge: Start small. Introduce emotional check-ins as a new family ritual. Let your kids see you naming your emotions and modeling resilience. Show them that emotional intelligence isn't about being perfect; it's about being present.

Because at the end of the day, the goal isn't just to raise emotionally intelligent kids—it's to raise emotionally resilient ones. And that starts with us.

The Power of Play

Dads and lawns—it's a love story as old as suburbia itself. The lines have to be straight, the grass perfectly trimmed, and heaven forbid anyone leaves a footprint on the freshly cut masterpiece. If there's one thing you can count on, it's that most dads will defend their lawns like generals protecting a fortress. "Stay off the grass!" might as well be etched into every dad's DNA

Harmon Killebrew, one of baseball's greatest legends, was known not just for his powerful swing but for the lessons he carried from his childhood. In his 1984 Hall of

Fame induction speech, Minnesota Twins legend Harmon Killebrew, known for his towering home runs and over 570 career blasts, shared a story that captured the essence of fatherhood and play. Reflecting on his father's approach to raising boys, Killebrew, who earned his place in Cooperstown for his powerful hitting and leadership, recalled:

> "My father used to play with my brother and me in the yard. Mother would come out and say, 'You're tearing up the grass.' Dad would reply, 'We're not raising grass, This is how I imagined Harmon telling his story."

The Day We Wrecked the Yard

The summer of 1944 in Payette, Idaho, was a scorcher. The kind of heat that made you grateful for shade and even more grateful for a cold drink. My brother Eugene and I were restless, though. No amount of lemonade could distract us from the endless hum of boredom. And when you're a young boy with energy to burn, boredom is practically a call to action.

Our dad, Harmon Sr., was sitting on the porch in his usual spot, reading the paper and watching us fidget like squirrels. He folded the paper neatly, set it aside, and stood up. "You boys look like you're about to combust," he said, a twinkle in his eye. "What do you say we play some ball?" Before he even finished the question, Eugene and I had bolted into the house, grabbing gloves, a bat, and our scuffed-up baseball.

Mom, of course, gave us her usual warning from the kitchen: "Don't tear up the yard!"We pretended not to hear her as we sprinted back outside. Dad laughed. "C'mon, let's see what you've got."

We turned our front yard into a makeshift baseball field. The sidewalk was first base, the rosebush was second, and an old bucket marked third. Dad pitched underhand, letting Eugene and me take turns trying to hit a ball that seemed to dart and curve more than it should've—because Dad had a knack for making even the simplest game feel like the World Series.

Eugene hit a line drive that sent me diving to the ground; my glove stretched out just in time to make the catch. Dust flew everywhere, and I could hear Mom groaning from inside the house. "You're tearing up the grass!" she called out, exasperated.

I expected Dad to stop the game, maybe call it quits, or at least tell us to be more careful. Instead, he looked at her, then back at us, and smiled. "We're not raising grass," he said, tossing the ball back to Eugene. "We're raising boys."

At its core, play is the language of childhood. Through play, children learn to interact with the world around them. This universal language offers a window into the unspoken, bridging gaps between worlds, thoughts, and emotions. For fathers, intentional play is not just an activity;

it's a dialogue—a way to communicate love, interest, and security to their children.

For years, I've watched fathers from a distance, unsure how to engage with their children while they play. My interpretation of that is quite simple: We're out of practice. At some point in life, you learn to have fun with your imagination or with other people. During your formative years, play became something that children do, and adults invested their time in hobbies, sports, or knowledge.

Learning how to play and play well with others are the building blocks of good team dynamics. You probably know one person who is a jokester or attention grabber. Phrases such as you play too much may be thrown around. Let's describe the fundamentals of play.

Play is

When children are in their formative years, playing is how and where you will learn about their feelings, dreams, problems, fears, and copious amounts of information that will make you a better parent. Jim Carry starred in a movie called Liar Liar, where his character was a lawyer who was divorcing his wife but had a son. Jim Carey's character in that movie would put his hand inside his jacket, and what would emerge would be this believed monster called " the claw," and his son would run all around the house trying not to be tickled by the claw.

Unstructured Play: Purposeful play is spontaneous and unscripted, focusing on short bursts of joyful interaction. These moments happen organically in the flow of daily life and are often lighthearted. They emphasize connection and fun without a specific agenda or set rules.

Examples:
Having a mini dance-off in the kitchen while preparing dinner. Turning bath time into an imaginative adventure with toy boats and bubbles.
They spontaneously raced each other to the car after school pickup.

Intentional Play: Intentional play involves creating or introducing activities with a specific purpose in mind. These activities are designed to foster emotional connection, teach a life skill, or encourage creativity. It requires forethought and planning, as the goal is to create a meaningful and lasting impact through structured interaction.

Examples:
Teaching teamwork by organizing a family board game night. Exploring creativity through an art project where both father and child collaborate on a painting.
Encouraging responsibility by planting and caring for a garden together.

Purposeful Play: Structured play involves activities where clear rules, boundaries, or time limits are established. While the child may initiate these activities, the father provides guidance and moderation, ensuring the experience is both fun and constructive. This type of play helps children learn discipline, boundaries, and teamwork.

Examples:
Setting up a weekly soccer game with family or friends, with designated teams and rules.
Hosting a LEGO-building challenge where each participant has a theme to follow within a set time.
Playing a video game together while discussing strategies and ensuring time is managed appropriately.

Goal-Oriented Play: Goal-oriented play uses activities as a vehicle for teaching important lessons or addressing sensitive topics in a safe, engaging way. It goes beyond simple enjoyment, turning play into a tool for emotional, social, or cognitive development.

Examples:
Using a puzzle-solving game to teach problem-solving skills and patience.
Role-playing scenarios (e.g., a customer and shopkeeper) to practice communication and empathy.
Playing a game of pretend to introduce concepts like sharing, consent, or fairness (e.g., "Let's practice taking turns with the treasure chest").

Play plants the seeds of passion.

Fathers, sons, and brothers are on a quest to find hidden treasure. This might sound like a story from a book, but for the team behind *The Curse of Oak Island*, it is a real adventure that has fascinated viewers for years. While the excitement of finding gold draws people in, the true value lies in the friendships and bonds that develop through their shared experiences.

Rick and Marty Lagina epitomize this bond. Rick's childhood fascination with Oak Island's mystery, sparked by a 1965 Reader's Digest article, became a lifelong dream. Decades later, Marty, the pragmatic engineer, helped turn that dream into a full-scale family project. Together, their contrasting personalities—Rick's optimism and Marty's practicality—forge a partnership built on mutual respect and the joy of working side by side.

Their collaboration extended to Marty's son, Alex, who brings fresh energy and engineering expertise to the team. Watching Alex learn from his father and uncle and contribute to the legacy they're building is as rewarding as any artifact unearthed. Similarly, Craig Tester and his stepson, Jack Begley, find meaning in continuing the work of Craig's late son, Drake, ensuring his memory remains woven into their quest.

And then there's Gary Drayton, the exuberant met-al-detecting expert who once brought his daughter, Anya, to join the search. That day of treasure hunting wasn't just about artifacts—it was about creating memories they'd cherish forever.

What ties all these relationships together is a shared sense of play. From Rick's awe over an ancient artifact to Gary's celebratory "bobby dazzlers," the team's joy in the process underscores a profound truth: the greatest treasure isn't buried—it's found in the connections we nurture along the way.

The fathers, sons, brothers, and stepfathers of The Curse of Oak Island remind us that life's most meaningful adventures are those we share with the people we love. Their legacy isn't measured in gold but in the bonds they've built and the memories they've created.

Playtime Chronicles

Understanding how play changes over time allows us, as fathers, to engage with our children in ways that support their development at every stage. Play is not just for children. It is a lifelong practice—one that builds confidence, creativity, and connection at every turn.

Infancy (0-2 years)

In infancy, play is centered around sensory exploration and motor development. Newborns and babies engage in play through their senses, such as touching, tasting, and seeing. During this stage, play is spontaneous and instinctive, helping infants develop foundational skills such as object permanence and motor control. Simple interactions like peek-a-boo, rattles, and soft toys stimulate curiosity and early social bonding.

How play manifests: Infants explore their world by grasping objects, making sounds, and reacting to visual and tactile stimuli. This play helps strengthen the parent-child bond and promotes early emotional and social development.

Toddlerhood (2-4 years)

As toddlers, children begin to engage in more active, imaginative, and independent play. This stage is marked by physical activity, pretend play, and the use of toys that foster creativity. Through play with others, toddlers practice coordination, language development, and basic social skills.

How play manifests: Play often involves mimicking adults or creating simple fantasy worlds, such as pretending to cook or care for a doll. Playdates with peers introduce early socialization, while games like building blocks or drawing enhance cognitive and motor development.

Early Childhood (4-7 years)

At this age, children develop more structured, inter-active forms of play. They begin to create more complex storylines in their pretend games and develop rules for simple games. Play at this stage becomes crucial for learning cooperation, problem-solving, and emotional regulation.

How play manifests: Children play in groups more often, sharing toys and navigating social roles. Games with clear rules, such as tag, board games, and simple sports, teach them about teamwork, fairness, and competition. Pretend play becomes more elaborate, often mimicking real-world scenarios like running a store or playing house

Middle Childhood (7-12 years)

Play during middle childhood shifts toward games that require logic, strategy, and more complex social interactions. Children explore competitive games, group sports, and board games, which introduce the concepts of rules, fairness, and structured outcomes.

How play manifests: Play becomes more focused on collaboration and competition. Children participate in organized sports or group activities, like soccer or chess, that demand strategic thinking and teamwork. Imaginative play continues but with more structure, often related to their interests or hobbies, such as video games or collecting items.

Adolescence (13-18 years)

During adolescence, play evolves to include more complex and sophisticated activities that demand deeper strategic thinking, problem-solving, and collaboration.

simple games. Play at this stage becomes crucial for learning cooperation, problem-solving, and emotional regulation.

How play manifests: Children play in groups more often, sharing toys and navigating social roles. Games with clear rules, such as tag, board games, and simple sports, teach them about teamwork, fairness, and competition. Pretend play becomes more elaborate, often mimicking real-world scenarios like running a store or playing house

Middle Childhood (7-12 years)

Play during middle childhood shifts toward games that require logic, strategy, and more complex social interactions. Children explore competitive games, group sports, and board games, which introduce the concepts of rules, fairness, and structured outcomes.

How play manifests: Play becomes more focused on collaboration and competition. Children participate in organized sports or group activities, like soccer or chess, that demand strategic thinking and teamwork. Imaginative play continues but with more structure, often related to their interests or hobbies, such as video games or collecting items.

Adolescence (13-18 years)

During adolescence, play evolves to include more complex and sophisticated activities that demand deeper strategic thinking, problem-solving, and collaboration.

Task-Oriented

"Just like in our game, if someone's eyes does something ... it makes you uncomfortable, like touching you in a way you don't like, you can say 'No!' And if you feel ... unsure, you can always talk to me or Mom, and we'll help."

Intentional

Can we play tickle monster after dinner?" The father agrees ... our ... boundaries by saying, "Okay, the tickle monster can play for 10 minutes ... and then it's time for a break ..." ... up for bed." During the game, the father might let the child "defend" the tickle monster, ... encouraging them to develop leadership and decision-making skills.

Purposeful

Here comes the tickle monster, but don't worry—you can say "stop" and the monster will pause." This not only builds excitement but also lets the game work for ... everyone involved and boundaries during play.

Unintentional

"Oh no! The tickle monster is hiding in your sleeve!" and begins a playful tickle attack. This ... moment of lighthearted interaction, reinforcing the bond in a fun, low-pressure manner.

153

Pause & Reflect

How often do you play with your kids within a week? Enter time in minutes?

Sunday	Monday	Tuesday	Wednes-day	Thurs-day	Friday	Saturday

Consider the response above and provide examples for each category listed below.

Category	Example 1	Example 2	Example 3
Unstruc-tured			
Pur-poseful			

Inten- tional			
Goal Orient- ed			

Do you feel like the time you spend with your kids is enough?

How do you want your kids to remember their childhood with you?

What childhood game that you remember do you want your kids to learn?

What have you learned about your kids through play that has made you a better parent?

Have you noticed anything in this chapter that might prevent you from playing with your child, such as past experiences, trauma, or cultural differences?

"Hard times create strong men. Strong men create good times. Good times create weak men, weak men create hard times."

– G. Michael Hopf, Those Who Remain.

Fostering Lifelong Learning

I first read this quote in 2022 when the world was struggling to regain a new semblance of normalcy. An unintended by-product of the entire world shutting down for almost two years was the amount of new skills people acquired because of the time we had to invest. With an enormous amount of free time, people around the world started to scratch things off their bucket lists. Here are a few items people around the world dove into.

- Embracing Creativity: Baking, painting, and learning musical instruments.
- Digital Dexterity: Video conferencing became the norm, and many learned to navigate new platforms for work, education, and entertainment.
- Culinary Confidence: Restaurants were closed or limited, so people embraced home cooking. There was a rise in online recipe searches and exploration of new cuisines.
- Domestic Wellness: Confined spaces meant a new focus on creating a comfortable and healthy home environment. People learned skills like gardening, home organization, and DIY projects.
- Fitness Flexibility: Gyms were closed, but fitness didn't stop. There was a boom in online workout programs, home exercise routines, and outdoor activities like running and cycling. 29

Learning a new hobby or skill allowed anyone with an interest to instantly belong, become a part of a community, and be able to share their success and failures within that community. They found support, purpose, and success in a time when the world was surrounded by conflict and solitude.

The Great Diaper Rebellion

At the peak of our diaper-changing enterprise,

we were hitting an eye-watering 670 diaper changes per month. That's right—670. For almost four months straight, we averaged 22 diapers a day, every day. Let that sink in for a moment. We were basically running a 24/7 factory for diaper disposal. Words can't quite capture the overwhelming concern, the mounting cost, and the sheer speed with which I dreamed of potty training our girls.

But dreams, as they say, don't always align with reality. Potty training was going to be a long process, and like most things in parenting, it required patience—a virtue I was desperately trying to cultivate. I was ambitious, stubborn, and more than a little determined to make it work. I mean, if we could survive the chaos of the NICU and eight weeks of bed rest, surely I could handle a little potty training. Right?

Wrong.

Our first attempt was, let's just say, unsuccessful. For weeks, I failed to instill a basic understanding of the process in our girls. There were plenty of accidents, a lot of frustration, and one unfortunate incident involving a potty training seat and a forgotten juice box. It wasn't pretty.

Enter: Annie, the Potty Whisperer

Thankfully, my wife, Annie, stepped in with a method she'd discovered on one of the many mom blogs she followed. It was a three-day potty training boot camp that promised results. I was skeptical, but desperate times call for desperate measures.

I'll spare you the full details—you can find the exact method we used in the attached resources, but let me just say it worked. Within a week, we saw progress. Within two weeks, we saw significant progress. And within a month, we were diaper-free during the day. It was like being handed a golden ticket to freedom.

But potty training wasn't just about getting rid of diapers. It was also about learning how to clean themselves properly. And as a man, let me tell you—this was a learning curve for me, too. I didn't fully appreciate the importance of wiping front to back until we dealt with several UTIs early on. That's a lesson you only need to learn once (or twice) before it's burned into your brain for eternity.

As we transitioned out of diapers, I noticed the amount of toilet paper, specifically, the amount of toilet paper. When I tell you we went through rolls like wildfire, I'm not exaggerating. Before potty training, a single toilet paper roll would last us three to four weeks. Post-potty training? We were flying through double-ply like it was Halloween candy.

At one point, I made the mistake of trying to cut costs by downgrading to a cheaper brand. Parents, let me tell you—never do this. There is no greater betrayal than reaching for toilet paper only to feel your finger poke through the delicate, gas-station-grade one-ply tissue. It's a level of discomfort a petty person wishes on their enemy. Naturally, teaching the girls how to use the right amount of toilet paper became a priority. That's when my next parenting idea was born.

The Balloon Exercise

It was October 2019, just past the girls' birthday, when I stumbled across a series of videos from South Korea, Japan, and China. The kids in these videos were doing everything from dribbling basketballs with one hand to performing intricate martial arts routines. But what really caught my eye was a clip of a preschool teacher using two balloons strapped to the back of a chair to teach her students how to properly clean themselves after using the bathroom. It was genius. And it was exactly what we needed.

So, one afternoon, I gathered three chairs that were the perfect height for our girls. I attached two pink balloons to the back of each chair for a little extra encouragement and brought out some carefully measured squares of toilet paper. First, I demonstrated the process—counting out the squares, folding them, and mimicking a proper wipe. Then, it was their turn.

To my surprise, they took to it right away. And, because I couldn't resist documenting the moment, I recorded the entire exercise on my phone. What I didn't know at the time was that those videos would take on a life of their own.

Two months later, I received a call from a casting director in California. She introduced herself and explained that she was working on a project spotlighting Black fathers who were doing extraordinary things with their kids. The project was produced by Will Smith and hosted by KevOnStage.
I thought she had the wrong number.

She didn't.

Our toilet paper demonstration video garnered attention on social media, and someone on her team had flagged it. She asked for my permission to use the video for their project, and I didn't hesitate for a second.

That phone call was more than an opportunity to be featured on a show. It was a reminder of the power of play in parenting. Something as simple as a balloon and some toilet paper had turned into a teaching moment, a bonding experience, and now, a story worth sharing.

Potty training is one of those pivotal early milestones that mark the shift from dependency to independence. It's messy, frustrating, and, at times, feels downright impossible. Yet, it's also a profound reminder of how deeply our children rely on us—not only for guidance through the small hurdles of life but also for the connection that reassures them they're not navigating it alone.

The truth is, play isn't just about fun. It's about building trust, fostering communication, and creating memories that will last long after the diapers are gone. Whether it's a silly toilet paper exercise or an impromptu dance party in the living room, these moments are the foundation of secure attachment. They remind our children that we are present. That we see them. That we are invested in their growth—not just as parents but as partners in their journey. And sometimes, those moments are enough to get you a call from Hollywood.

Teaching is a skill that needs to be honed. It is neither easy nor quick but requires patience, determination, listening, understanding, and agility. Individually, those traits are challenging. Add the complexity of your doppelganger powers to uniquely frustrate you, and it can seem like a never-ending task. No matter where you fall on the line of fatherhood, I want you to list the most important concepts, lessons, morals, or ideas that you want your kids to have.

Example:
It was always very important that I teach my kids how to have a healthy relationship with food.

Have you ever sat down with your team to create a strategy to achieve a goal? Where do you start? What objectives do you want to accomplish? What tasks need to be completed to achieve those goals? How do those objectives relate to the mission or vision of your team? Remove your work, team, business, and all the other noise.

This is your fatherly strategy session with your private, professional dad coach. Don't make this hard. Start where you feel inspiration.

Pillars of development

The Pillars of Development in the context of fatherhood are foundational categories that encompass the essential aspects and skills a father aims to instill in their children. These pillars serve as guiding principles for nurturing well-rounded individuals who are prepared to navigate life's complexities with resilience, empathy, and understanding.

Here are a few pillars you may want to consider.
- Character and Values Life Skills
- The World around us
- Emotional Intelligence
- Finding Their Passion
- Resilience and Adaptability
- Creativity and
- Exploration financial literacy
- The importance of Family Time Management
- Leadership and Responsibility Communication and Social Skills The World around us
- Problem-solving and Critical Thinking
- Finding Their Passion
- Health and Wellness
- Conflict Resolution

- Collaboration and Teamwork
- Environmental Stewardship
- Spiritual Growth and Mindfulness
- And many more.

Physical activity and sportsmanship are just two examples of how the Pillars of Development can be applied in real life.

These foundational categories help guide the lessons, skills, and values we pass on to our children, ensuring they grow into resilient, empathetic, and well-rounded individuals. As you reflect on the pillars that resonate most with you, consider which characteristics you want your child to embody and how they might apply these principles in their daily lives.

On to the exercise.

Pilar of Development	Characteristic	Scenario
Health and Wellness	A healthy relationship with food	Display self-control in the face of loads of candy during parties or Halloween.

I learned late in life how to have a healthy relationship with food. Regardless of the gender of my children, I wanted to teach them how to have a positive and healthy relationship with food.

Let's activate our creative side.

Imagine your life 1-5 years from now. Visualizing the future helps you identify the moments and activities that matter most in building your relationship with your children. Take a moment to reflect on these questions:

- How do you imagine spending your Saturday afternoons?
- What do your summers look like as a family?
- Where are you going when it's warm outside?
- What are you doing when it's cold and rainy?
- What hobby or activity are you doing to foster and develop your bond with your child?
- What activities or hobbies do you wish your child would want to share with you?

After reflecting, jot down your thoughts to uncover common themes or priorities. These insights can guide you in shaping intentional moments together."

Pilar of Development	Characteristic	Scenario
The broad domain or area of focus in a child's growth, such as Health, Emotional Intelligence, etc.	A specific value, skill, or principle you want your child to embody within the pillar.	A real-life, age-appropriate situation where the characteristic can be applied or practiced.

Pause & Reflect

What did you become aware of as you compare your lists together?

The Art of Attach- ments Styles

At just 20 weeks, Annie carried a belly rivaling what most expectant mothers show at full term, so we decided to share our news with the world. It felt like the right thing to do. After weeks of uncertainty, challenges, and medical appointments filled with daunting possibilities, we had weathered the most harrowing storms thus far. Optimism was starting to replace fear. For the first time in months, it felt like we could celebrate.

This sense of celebration, however, came with a bittersweet farewell. We had to part ways with Dr. Branning as our delivery doctor. The hospital equipped to handle high-risk pregnancies like ours didn't permit him to operate there. It was a loss we felt deeply. Dr. Branning had been more than a doctor; he had been our Marco Polo through the uncharted waters of this journey, guiding us through the dreary nights of uncertainty with steady reassurance. We thanked him for helping us navigate the storm and braced ourselves for the next chapter.

Enter Dr. Burt—a man who immediately brought light to our new reality. Friendly, jovial, and, most importantly, someone who laughed at all of my jokes, Dr. Burt quickly became the steady presence we needed as the road ahead grew more challenging.

Dr. Burt tempered our growing excitement with a dose of pragmatism. Babies B and C were still at high risk, and Annie's mobility would have to be restricted for the remainder of the pregnancy. Bed rest was no longer a precaution; it was a mandate. So, just past the halfway mark of a typical 40-week pregnancy, Annie moved into the hospital.

The sweltering Texas summer, already unbearable for anyone, was particularly unkind to a woman carrying 60 pounds of baby, fluids, and hope in her stomach. The hospital became our new home. Annie was monitored two to three times a day with ultrasounds, ensuring that Babies B and C's umbilical cords didn't tangle and that any emergencies could be met with immediate care.

Oddly enough, I started nesting during this time. Every morning, I worked; every afternoon, I was at home prepping the house; and every evening, I sat with Annie at the hospital—rinse and repeat for eight straight weeks. With each passing day, my excitement built to a fever pitch. I couldn't wait to meet them, hold them, and hear their cries. It consumed my every waking moment.

The delivery was scheduled for exactly 32 weeks— September 14th at noon. Annie and I had reached the pinnacle of our anticipation. I was determined to make the day as unforgettable as possible. If a wedding day is a woman's day, then delivery day, I reasoned, belonged to me.

I threw myself into the occasion. I made custom t-shirts with "ABCD Day" emblazoned across the front. Armed with a DSLR camera around my neck and a GoPro strapped to my head, I resembled a documentarian on a mission. Nothing would escape my lens.

But beneath the playful exterior, I had one non-negotiable request: Annie and I needed time alone with the babies before introducing them to anyone else. The hospital's setup meant the babies would be delivered in a room near a separate waiting area and then transported down a short corridor to the NICU. I had made it clear to both families that there would be no stops for pictures or visitors—we were going directly to the NICU. But, as with most family requests, this fell on deaf ears.

In the delivery room, Annie clutched my hand tightly as she was prepped for surgery. Her nerves were palpable. Free from the 60 pounds she'd been carrying, she would finally meet the three little souls who had turned our lives upside down. Yet the anesthesia made her anxious, and as the medical team bustled around us, she looked at me with wide, determined eyes. She said clearly, "Knock me the hell out."

The anesthesiologist hesitated. "Don't you want to see your babies when they're delivered?"

" I'll see them later," Annie replied. "Knock me out. Now." The team carried on, and I stayed by Annie's side as two OBGYNs began the C-section. I had promised I wouldn't look directly at the surgical field—both for Annie's privacy and my own faintheartedness. My GoPro was perfectly positioned to capture the moment without me witnessing anything too graphic.

"One minute to the first baby!" the male OBGYN announced.

I rose with my camera, bracing for the moment I'd

been dreaming about for months. Instead, what I saw was an image that burned into my brain forever: Annie's abdomen was open to the world, her body breathing steadily as the surgeons worked. I swallowed hard, steadied myself, and didn't pass out.

The first baby, Alexa, was pulled out and whisked to her station. She cried immediately, and I felt a rush of relief so profound I thought I might collapse. They offered me a chance to hold her, but I declined. I wasn't ready to take the risk of dropping her in front of 24 medical professionals.

Then came Brielle, whose delivery was interrupted by her twin sister Camila—clinging to her ankle as if refusing to let go. The room chuckled as Camila was gently pushed back in for a moment. When Brielle was finally delivered, the doctor gasped.

"Look at this," he said, motioning for me to come closer. Brielle and Camila's umbilical cords were knotted tightly together—a miracle they had survived this long. Dr. Burt later told us that if we had waited even a week longer, they might not have made it.

Finally, Camila entered the world—late, dramatic, and as full of life as her sisters. The room buzzed with activity, and all three girls were safely delivered as the medical team assessed their vitals. My most critical task was ahead: ensuring the girls made it to the NICU without interruption. As soon as the double doors swung open, I became a human barricade, blocking curious family members from catching even a glimpse. This moment belonged to Annie, me, and our daughters.

Once the girls were settled in their incubators, I finally exhaled. The nurses completed their checks, tucked them into their tiny beds, and encouraged us to begin the most important task of all: skin-to-skin bonding.

There's something deeply sacred about those moments when your newborn lays against your chest. Their tiny bodies, barely three pounds each, rested on us as we whispered, hummed, and let them feel the rhythms of our hearts. For Alexa and Brielle, it was easy. They snuggled in without hesitation, their tiny hands clutching at my skin. But Camila was different. She was restless, almost resistant, and it broke my heart. Whenever I held her, she squirmed and fussed, making me question if I was doing something wrong.

Instead of giving up, I doubled down. I came to the NICU earlier each day, determined to win her over. I whispered stories into her tiny ears, sang softly, and told her everything I hoped for in her future. Slowly, almost imperceptibly, she began to relax. She stopped fighting. One day, she gripped my chest with tiny fingers, and I knew we had connected.

Those early bonding moments—of holding, whispering, and simply being present—laid the foundation for something much deeper: secure attachment.

In the coming chapters, we'll explore what it means to create this kind of connection with your children. Attachment isn't just about the physical act of holding them; it's about building a sense of safety, trust, and love that shapes their emotional well-being for years to come. Looking back, I realize those NICU days weren't just about survival—they were about learning how to be present, listen, and show up for my daughters in ways that would define our relationship for the rest of our lives.

Because, in the end, fatherhood isn't about perfection—it's about connection. Connection begins with presence.

In the canvas of fatherhood, if there's one stroke that defines the masterpiece, it's the art of forming secure attachments. This invisible thread weaves through our children's hearts, crafting a tapestry of trust, safety, and unwavering love. It turns a simple hug into a haven, a laugh into a lifeline, and a shared silence into a symphony of understanding.

But these bonds don't form by accident. They are created intentionally through the moments we choose to show up, listen, and respond to our children's needs with empathy and care.

Secure attachments aren't just emotional concepts; they're the foundation for a child's resilience, self-esteem, and capacity to navigate the world with confidence.

This chapter isn't just about understanding attachment styles; it's about anchoring our children in the serene assurance that they are loved, valued, and understood. My goal is to give you both the knowledge and the tools to take purposeful action. Psychologists have identified how varying attachment styles influence a child's emotional development and relationships throughout their lives. By exploring these outcomes, we can better understand how to foster the secure attachments that will serve as the bedrock for their future.

Secure Attachment:

Secure attachments are the bedrock upon which children build their understanding of the world and their place within it. It's about being consistently present, not just in the physical sense but emotionally too. This is where a child feels safe, loved, and supported by their caregiver. They are comfortable exploring their surroundings and know their caregiver

Behavior
- Exploring their surroundings confidently, knowing their caregiver is nearby for support.
- Returning to the caregiver periodically to check-in or seek comfort.
- Expressing emotions freely and being easily comforted when upset.

Avoidant-Dismissive Attachment:

Individuals with this style prioritize independence and distance themselves from intimacy. They may be emotionally unavailable, dismissive of closeness, and appear cold or aloof.

Behavior
- Avoiding interaction with the caregiver, even after separation or stress.
- Playing independently without seeking comfort or acknowledgment.
- Suppressing emotions to maintain distance from the caregiver.

Disorganized Attachment:

This is the least common style and is characterized by inconsistent behavior. People with disorganized attachment may have a mixture of anxious and avoidant behaviors stemming from early experiences with unpredictable caregivers. They may struggle with emotional regulation and have difficulty managing closeness.

Behavior
- Exhibiting erratic behavior, like approaching the caregiver but then pulling away.
- Acting fearful or confused around the caregiver, sometimes freezing or hesitating.
- Difficulty managing emotions or seeking comfort due to

inconsistent caregiver responses.

What Does Attachment Look Like in Practical Terms?

Attachment styles shape how individuals relate to others, express emotions, and navigate closeness in relationships. Understanding these styles can help fathers recognize patterns in themselves and their children, offering opportunities to build healthier connections.

Secure Attachment

What it looks like:
- Confidence in relationships: Securely attached individuals trust others and feel comfortable giving and receiving love.
- Healthy independence: They can seek support when needed but are also comfortable being self-sufficient.
- Open communication: They are honest and transparent in expressing their emotions.
- Resilience in conflict: They approach disagreements calmly and work toward resolution.

How fathers can foster it:
- Be emotionally available: Respond to your child's needs with empathy and attentiveness.
- Encourage exploration: Create a safe base from which your child feels confident venturing into the world.
- Model healthy relationships: Show the balance in expressing emotions and resolving conflicts.

Anxious Attachment

What it looks like:

- The constant need for reassurance: Seeking frequent validation and worrying about being "good enough."
- Clingy behavior: Fear of abandonment leading to resistance to independence.
- Jealousy and possessiveness: Overly protective or suspicious of threats to relationships.
- Difficulty with intimacy: Craving closeness but avoiding vulnerability due to fear of rejection.

How fathers can address it:

- Offer consistent reassurance: Show unconditional love and emphasize their worth.
- Set boundaries gently: Encourage independence in a supportive, non-threatening way.
- Be patient: Acknowledge their fears and guide them toward trusting themselves and others.

Avoidant Attachment

What it looks like:

- Fear of intimacy and commitment: Avoiding emotional closeness or sabotaging relationships.
- Emotionally unavailable: Struggling to express feelings or prioritize relationships.
- Dismissive of closeness: Downplaying the importance of emotional connection.
- Appearing cold or aloof: Focusing on independence at

the expense of relationships.

How fathers can address it:
- Foster emotional safety: Normalize discussions about feelings and validate their emotions.
- Encourage gradual intimacy: Help them see the value of closeness without overwhelming them.
- Balance independence with connection: Celebrate their autonomy while reminding them of the strength in relationships.

Disorganized Attachment

What it looks like:
- Inconsistent behavior: Fluctuating between craving closeness and pushing others away.
- Difficulty regulating emotions: Intense emotional responses and struggles with managing feelings.
- Fearful of relationships: A mix of longing for connection and being terrified of vulnerability.

How fathers can address it:
- Provide stability: Consistently show up as a calm and reassuring presence.
- Teach emotional regulation: Help your child name, understand, and manage their feelings.
- Build trust: Create predictable routines and environments to reduce anxiety.

Pause & Reflect

Write about one consistent routine you share with your child (e.g., bedtime stories, weekend breakfasts). How does this routine strengthen your bond? What could you add or change to make it even more meaningful?

Think about a recent moment when you felt frustrated in front of your child. How did you react? What could you do differently next time to model calmness and patience?

List three ways you currently show your child they are safe and loved. Are there additional ways you can reinforce this message in your daily interactions?

Choose one attachment-building activity (e.g., playtime, heartfelt conversations, or listening without distractions). Schedule it into your week and reflect on the experience afterward.

Foundations of Trust and Connection

Consistency is Key

If there's one mantra that should echo through our actions as fathers, it's consistency. Children thrive on predictability, and it's in the routine bedtime stories, regular family dinners, and consistent acknowledgment of their feelings that they find a foundation of security. These rituals become the rhythm to which their sense of stability dances, shaping how they trust and connect with the world.

Become Legendary: Identify one daily ritual you can commit to— whether it's a bedtime story, a morning hug, or a weekly family activity. Your consistent presence is the cornerstone of their emotional safety.

Secure attachments are spoken in the language of love—a language that transcends words. It's in the eyes that light up when they walk into the room, the smile that celebrates their achievements, no matter how small, and the patience that meets their mistakes.

This love listens—not just to what is said but to what is left unsaid. It hears the silence in their sighs, reads the tension in their shoulders, and understands the quiet plea in their downcast gaze.

Become Legendary: Reflect on how you express love beyond words. Is your body language open and inviting? Do your eyes convey pride and acceptance? Small, consistent actions reinforce the love they feel.

Forming secure attachments doesn't mean shielding children from every hardship—it means being their safe haven. It's providing a space where they can explore, fail, and flourish, knowing they have a sanctuary to return to when they falter.

It's about giving them the freedom to stretch their

wings while assuring them that your steady presence will catch them if they fall.

Become Legendary: Create opportunities for your child to take risks and try new things. Celebrate their efforts, whether they succeed or stumble, and remind them they are always supported.

Children are astute observers, mirrors reflecting our attitudes and behaviors. How we handle stress, resolve conflicts, and express love becomes their template for relationships. By modeling secure attachment through our actions—showing patience in frustration, kindness in disagreements, and resilience in challenges—we teach them the dance of healthy emotional connections.

Become Legendary: Be mindful of how you navigate your relationships in their presence. What are you teaching them about love, respect, and self-control through your actions?

The Legacy of Secure Attachment

The legacy of forming secure attachments is profound and far-reaching. These early bonds are not just about comfort or connection in childhood—they become the blueprint for how children relate to themselves and others throughout their lives. Secure attachments instill a deep sense of self-worth and belonging, equipping children with the tools they need to thrive emotionally, socially, and even academically.

When children experience consistent love, empathy, and support, they develop an innate belief that they are worthy of care and affection. This belief serves as their foundation as they navigate the complexities of life. Securely attached children are more likely to venture confidently into the world, explore new opportunities, and take risks because they trust in their ability to overcome challenges.

What Legendary Fathers Do?

Being Present:

1. What it looks like: Carve out dedicated time to engage with your child without distractions. This could be as simple as playing a board game, having bedtime conversations, or taking a walk together.
2. The long-term impact: These moments of connection teach your child that they are a priority and lay the foundation for their confidence in relationships.

Offering Unconditional Love:

1. What it looks like: Respond with patience and empathy, even during challenging moments. When your child makes mistakes or expresses strong emotions, use these as opportunities to show them your love is unwavering.
2. The long-term impact: Your consistent reassurance fosters resilience, helping them feel secure even when

faced with adversity.

Creating Emotional Safety

1. What it looks like: Validate their feelings and encourage open communication. When they share their fears, dreams, or frustrations, listen actively and without judgment.
2. The long-term impact: By modeling emotional vulnerability, you teach your child to approach relationships with honesty and empathy.

Encouraging Exploration

1. What it looks like: Provide a secure base from which your child feels confident to explore the world. Cheer them on as they try new activities, and remind them that failure is a natural part of learning.
2. The long-term impact: This builds their independence and willingness to embrace new challenges, knowing they have your support.

Understanding Attachment Styles Across Life Stages

Attachment is the invisible thread that shapes how we connect with others, from our earliest days as infants to our relationships as adults. By understanding the four primary attachment styles—secure, anxious-preoccupied, avoidant-dismissive, and disorganized—we gain insight into how our children experience love, trust, and connection.
The table below breaks down how these attachment styles

manifest at different life stages, from infancy to adulthood. By identifying these patterns, you can better support your child's emotional growth and take intentional steps to nurture secure attachments.

Attachment Style	Definition	Baby (Birth - 1 Year)	5-Year-Old	10-Year-Old	Adult
Secure Attachment	Feels safe, loved, and supported by a caregiver. Explores surroundings confidently.	Easily comforted by a caregiver, explores freely.	Seeks comfort and feels secure in friendships.	Develops healthy, trusting relationships.	Maintains strong relationships and intimacy.
Anxious-Preoccupied	Craves reassurance and fears abandonment. May be clingy and jealous.	Needs frequent comfort separation anxiety.	Clingy with friends, worries about rejection.	Seeks constant validation and struggles with trust.	Difficulty with intimacy may be possessive.

Avoidant-Dismissive	Prioritizes independence and avoids intimacy. May be emotionally unavailable.	Avoids seeking comfort and may appear withdrawn.	Prefers solitude and struggles with the connection.	Focuses on independence and downplays relationships.	Difficulty forming deep connections, fears vulnerability
Disorganized Attachment	Inconsistent behavior is a mixture of anxious and avoidant tendencies.	Shows inconsistent behaviors and struggles emotionally.	Confused about closeness, craves connection	Unstable relationships struggle with trust.	They may have chaotic relationships and emotional struggles.

Establish a Legendary Legacy

Legacies often seem grand—empires built, records broken, dynasties forged. However, when you strip away the headlines and highlights, every legacy begins as a whisper—a small, intentional act that ripples through time.

Deion Sanders, known as "Prime Time," has built a

legacy as both a Hall of Fame athlete and a transformative coach. Now leading the University of Colorado football team, Sanders calls his current role "a father's dream."
Coaching his sons, Shedeur and Shilo, while his third son,
Deion Jr., documents every moment and his daughter,
Shelomi, offers unwavering support, Sanders shared: "Do
you know how much fun we have, man? Do you understand
that when we are on offense, I'm watching my son? When
we are on defense, I'm watching my son. Then, my son is
watching my sons. I can't have a bad day because I'm surrounded by family. This is a father's dream."

LeBron James, one of basketball's all-time greats,
dreams of playing alongside his son Bronny in the NBA.
Despite his championships and MVP titles, he considers this
aspiration among his proudest ambitions: "I need to be on
the floor with my boy. I've got to be on the floor with Bronny. That would be the greatest thing I've ever done in my
career."

These men, icons in their fields, remind us that legacies aren't forged in stats or accolades alone. They're built
in backyards, living rooms, and gyms. They grow from small
moments: a game of catch, quiet encouragement after a
setback, or shared dreams of what could be.

Tiny Seeds, Big Trees

Legacies are like oak trees, starting as tiny acorns.
You don't need fame or fortune to plant them—just consis-

tent effort and intentional moments with those you love.

Each of these stories demonstrates that legacies aren't about perfection—they're about presence. They're about showing up, listening, and modeling love, resilience, and purpose.

The First Step Is Yours

As a father, your legacy begins with the smallest of actions. Sit down for dinner with your kids. Ask them what made them smile today. Turn off the distractions and tune into their world.

Ask yourself:
- What small habit can I start today that will impact my family tomorrow?
- How can I use play, mentorship, or daily rituals to strengthen our bond?
- What values do I want to pass down, and how can I embody them?

Legacies grow through small, consistent actions. They're built when a father cheers at a soccer game in the rain, helps with homework after a long day, or simply listens without judgment.

The beauty of legacy is that it doesn't depend on where you start—it depends on the effort you're willing to invest. You don't need to be a professional athlete, a billionaire, or a president to make an impact. You already have the greatest tools: your time, your attention, and your love.

Plant tiny seeds today: teach your child to ride a bike, encourage them to try again after failure, or tell them you're proud of them. These moments shape who your children become—and through them, they shape the world.

As Deion Sanders says, "Don't just dominate the game. Change it."

In changing the game, you become more than just a father—you become a legendary father. A father whose presence, intentionality, and unwavering love create a ripple effect for generations. The game you change might not be on a field, but it will matter just the same.

Your legacy starts now. It starts small. But if you nurture it, it will grow into something extraordinary—something your children and their children will carry forward with pride.

That's the power of being a legendary father. That's the legacy worth leaving.

Fatherhood is a journey—why not wear it with pride?

Join the Elevate Fatherhood movement and rep the mindset of intentional, legendary dads. Whether you're building memories, leading with purpose, or just surviving the chaos, we've got the gear to match your mission.

Shop now at ElevateFatherhood.com and wear your legacy.

www.ingramcontent.com/pod-product-compliance
Lightning Source LLC
Jackson TN
JSHW022110220225
79461JS00001B/1